# The Ancient Path

*Hope for everyday life*
*from Psalm 23*

"Stand at the crossroads and look;
ask for the ancient paths,
ask where the good way is, and walk in it,
and you will find rest for your souls."
Jeremiah 6:16 (NIV)

**Craig Smith**
**Village2Village**

# CONTENTS

# PREFACE

The desk lamp in the sunroom remains the sole light source in our house this quiet Friday evening, and I am the only one still awake. My wife fell asleep earlier in the living room. Our youngest son, the only one of our three still living with us, retired to his room some time ago.

This is my favorite place to read and write. The desk is a small one, a replica of an old World War II field desk, and is positioned on the only wall in the room that doesn't have windows. The other three walls are covered by large floor-to-ceiling windows (which are currently opened wide allowing the sounds and scents of the surrounding woods to enter into the room).

The south side overlooks a sloping front yard and joins a meadow of approximately ten acres before reaching a tree-covered hillside bordering the far side of the field, and the north and west sides look out into the natural surrounding of wooded landscapes.

In the morning hours or at dusk it is not uncommon to see deer, squirrels, rabbits, a dozen or so varieties of birds, or catch a glance of an opossum, raccoon, fox, and occasionally even a coyote.

On the desk before me is one of my older Bibles. Its black leather cover is worn and frayed, and the binding is giving way, but it is my favorite one to read from on days like this. It is currently opened to Psalm 23. To the right of it is a plain brown spiral notebook, a good writing pen, and just eighteen inches away a steaming hot cup of Starbucks® House blend coffee resting on a wooden coaster with a cork center.

The only sounds from outside are those created by a breeze lightly stirring the leaves on the trees and the various nocturnal creatures inhabiting the woods surrounding our house.

The chorus provided by the green tree frogs and crickets is most prominent and consistent, but every once in a while the hoot of an owl or the call of a whippoorwill dominates. The tones and rhythms are so pleasant they almost lull me to sleep.

Inside it is still and peaceful. The sound of my pen gliding across the paper is the primary sound, followed by the steady ticking rhythm of the second hand of a small cast-metal clock occupying the opposite side of the desk from the lamp.

My day began in this room early this morning. Except for a few brief strolls outdoors, I have spent the entire time reading, writing, and occasionally strumming my guitar. Peaceful...yes. Very, very peaceful indeed.

At this point you might be thinking, *This guy has an incredibly simple, stress free life.* Unfortunately, that is not the case.

Sure, it appears that way, but the truth is that I seldom get to enjoy this room and its atmosphere of solitude. The day I just described is actually a rare one because I reside in the same battleground of busyness as most of the people in the "industrial world". I succumb to its many distractions far too often.

Overload is my constant enemy—an adversary energized by distressing world events, worries over the spiraling economy, and a lack of self-discipline. Most painful of all, my struggle with the daily grind has produced a short-sightedness marked by my neglect to invest time and resources on the *truly valuable things*—those things that bring meaning and health to the heart.

I get distracted by the continuous flood of information bytes passing by me during the course of any given day via the marvelous broadband technological advances developed to "enhance" my lifestyle.

I once read an excerpt from a study conducted in the 1960's predicting "the average American lifestyle" in the early 1990's as a result of increased assistance via computer technology. Some of the conclusions were a shorter workweek, increased productivity, and a substantial decrease in stress within our culture....

Hmmm? A slight miscalculation may have occurred. I wonder just how much more time and programming is required before we reach this technology-driven nirvana?

Writer Brennan Manning once said, "Our lives in the global village have grown overly complex and crowded. New obligations grow overnight like Jack's beanstalk. Our days become a never-ending succession of appointments, committee meetings, burdens, and responsibilities."

Jesus promised us peace and joy, but I think very few actually take Him up on the offer and live it out, including most of us who claim to be His followers.

Meanwhile, we are weighed down by bulging appointment calendars, increased activity, and seemingly endless life-juggling distractions. How many times in casual conversation have you asked people how they're doing, only to hear these responses: "I'm busier than I have ever been" or "I am wrapped around the axle in overdrive"? Okay, you probably haven't heard the last one lately.

"Busy" is good if it truly produces life. Unfortunately, there is probably much more "wood, hay and stubble" cluttering our lives than we are willing to admit—or more importantly—more than we are bold enough to discard and change.

The foundation of our stress and worry stems from one primary root: the failure to carve out proper rest and quiet time. This is the vital quality time that restores and refuels us mentally, physically, and spiritually, not just time spent surfing the web or socializing on Facebook. For proof, simply scan a few shelves under the "emotional health" category in a local bookstore; listen to some talk radio programs, or review some articles on the declining quality of life.

The trouble is that our Creator hardwired us to fully reach our greatest potential in life *only* as we spend quality time with Him, the designer and master craftsman of humanity.

When we discover this, embrace it, and incorporate it into the fabric of our inner being, a wonderful metamorphosis occurs...*we experience life as it was intended*.

Genuine trust leads us to peace, rest, hope, and joy. These qualities provide the ingredients for better mental, spiritual, and physical wholeness.

In brief, time spent with and trusting God leads to real life, *zoe* life, the Greek word used to describe the life that comes from God. This "God-kind-of-life" can only be experienced by entering into an ongoing relationship with Him. He is the singular source for *zoe* life.

There is a narrow path that leads to this abundant life. It is an ancient path, but a proven one. It was established for all to discover. Unfortunately, only a minority of people choose to follow the trail.

Our focus for *The Ancient Path* and its companion music is simple: We want to reacquaint you with an old friend. We tap the truths found in a song of antiquity and disclose its premise. We seek to expose the One who desires to lead you and me to places that are good for our lives. We aim to re-introduce, or perhaps, to introduce you for the first time to the One called the Shepherd of our souls. We are shining a light on the path used by all who follow Him. He is the perfect friend who leads you to *more* than merely a passing experience of peace and rest. He is the *Way* to life.

Winston Churchill once said, "The further backward you look, the further forward you can see."[1] If you are willing to pause and look for a moment, an ancient path is waiting to be discovered. If you dare to step out and follow its course, it possesses the power to generate a fruitful and fulfilling life, totally opposite of one that is pointless, dulling, and draining of life!

Honestly, I feel I am an odd emissary for this venture, for the very message I bring is the one I seek.

Craig Smith

# INTRODUCTION

Few portions of scripture are as familiar to so many as The 23rd Psalm. Even those who are not very well acquainted with the Bible often recognize it when they hear it quoted or read.

It is one of many songs the Jewish King David composed during his lifetime. It is a flawless and beautiful song, with a theme of unwavering trust and hope in the Lord as his shepherd, and of the place of peace to which he is led. His song is simple, but it reveals deep and timeless truths pointing to a path available to all of us.

This musical prose is one of the great landmarks in God's precious life-giving Word, and to read it is like gazing at the map of a treasured city awaiting personal exploration.

First, you locate its main thoroughfares, and seek the familiar cornerstones that have long established its fame and reputation for countless generations of humanity. Yet, those are not the only places that widen the eyes and warm the heart. For many other less obvious places exist as well, lying quietly in want of discovery and offering additional comfort and fulfillment to its guests and seekers.

A few years ago, my wife and I took a trip to historic Williamsburg, Virginia. We had wanted to visit that city for some time because of its rich history and reputation. As with most vacation getaways, I mapped out the "must sees" first. We saw the sights and snapped a few photos to help us re-live the key moments of the past; then we began searching for some quaint out-of-the-way places in the region. We knew they must exist, though they were, perhaps, not as obvious.

As we strolled along one of the main streets, I noticed a small humble sign that managed to stir my curiosity. Its brief message was bolstered by a small black arrow pointing to an old bread shop. Even before we saw the sign, we could smell the alluring fragrance of fresh yeast bread in the oven.

We followed a narrow pathway between two buildings that opened into a small cobblestone patio. There, tucked quietly off a key thoroughfare, we found a wonderful old colonial baker's shop that produced fresh baked goods exactly as they were made in an era dating to the founding of the township. It was a hidden gem screened from the primary avenue. It still stands out in my memory as one of the favorite "finds" of the trip.

Psalm 23 possesses similar attributes, but on a much greater scale. It is one of the most quoted and recognized sacred texts common to the Jewish and Christian faiths; and it offers several quiet byways of truth when examined closely. Within its brief length you find the varied fragrances of Kingdom life and the ingredients for peace, fulfillment, and rest for the soul.

Charles Spurgeon referred to Psalm 23 as the "Pearl of Psalms." Scholar F.B. Meyer said: "… [The 23rd Psalm is] an oasis in the desert; it is a bower on a hill of arduous climbing; it is a grotto in a scorching noon; it is a sequestered arbor for calm and heavenly meditation; it is one of the most holy places in the temple of Scripture."[2]

As with our discovery of the little bakeshop in Williamsburg, there are numerous special places in this psalm awaiting discovery, places to which the Holy Spirit draws us using the fresh scent of the Bread of Heaven.

This psalm is home to a host of refreshing, simple, wonderful, and comforting words—genuine life-giving words. They are serene as a stream passing through a meadow during a peaceful summer rain. Quiet and refreshing as the first frost of early fall, bringing composure to the heart, clarity to the mind, and certainty to the soul. They reveal the sureness of the faithful guardian.

Spurgeon said of Psalm 23, "What a nightingale is among birds, that is this divine ode among the Psalms, for it has sung sweetly in the ear of many a mourner in his night of weeping, and has bidden him hope for a morning joy."[3]

Some of my most valued spiritual moments over the years have been those of purposed solitude, when I distanced myself from the activity of the average day in exchange for a withdrawal to seclusion accompanied only by a Bible, paper, pen, and occasionally a guitar.

I can only imagine what it was like for David to have penned and sung this psalm under the guidance of God's hand. He was at once a shepherd, a warrior, and a king.

As king, he bore the weighty responsibilities of ruling a nation. What was a typical day like for him? How many daily conflicts, distractions, and difficulties did he face? Was it a challenge for him to escape the demands of his duties for quiet time?

When I read this psalm, I picture David as one who had reached a deep level of communion, of careful contemplation, and perhaps most importantly, of resolve. He had absorbed into his being a most profound and abiding trust in God, and it deeply affected his life.

Regardless of our own individual careers, gifts, or positions; regardless of the demands upon us with all of the accompanying responsibilities and frequent diversions, we must wisely listen and respond to the beckoning call of the Holy Spirit.

He invites us to come, to linger within the solace of this great psalm.

Soak in the wealth waiting within the lines of this minstrel-poet's work. For under God's divine thoughts, this humble shepherd-king created a masterpiece for the heart and soul of human kind.

> *"Come hither, weary ones, restless ones, heavy laden ones;*
> *sit down in the cool calm resort,*
> *whilst the music of its rhythm charms away the thoughts that*
> *break your peace."*[4]

There is a well-marked, but ancient path of peace for us to follow.

> *"Come hither…"*

# CHAPTER ONE

## The Divine Guardian

*"The Lord is my Shepherd, I shall not want"*

I always enjoy exploring and walking in forests and wooded areas. For me, few things can equal the experience of strolling along a tree-covered hillside or walking through an isolated valley with a good creek winding through it on a sunny day in the spring or fall.

As a young boy, I anxiously waited to reach the required age to join the Scouting program sponsored by Shawnee Presbyterian Church, which was just a couple of blocks away from my childhood home in west Louisville, Kentucky.

My primary motive for joining the Scouts was my love for camping and hiking, and for every opportunity I could grab so I could go out into the countryside and woods.

On more than one occasion each summer, Troop 91 held week-long camping trips at Brown County State Park in Nashville, Indiana. I looked forward to those trips more than any other activity of the troop.

I still treasure the memories of waking up extra early for a big camp breakfast of homemade pancakes, fresh eggs, and bacon cooked on two huge propane Coleman® camp grills. Just the smell and sound of the bacon sizzling in the big cast iron skillet would draw me from the warmth and comfort of my sleeping bag to peek through the flaps of the old army surplus two-man canvas tent. I just had to see if a line was forming at the "mess tent."

After breakfast I would pack enough gear for the day and join a few dozen other guys before we piled into pick-up truck beds and crammed into cars for the drive to the trailhead where each day's hike started.

## The Trailhead

The journey was always adventurous and fun, and it was usually educational and rewarding in some way. The treasured vest holding all of those hard-earned patches now hangs at the far end of a rack in my closet—hidden from view. I tend to forget it is there until my wife decides our closet is due for a good cleaning. In the process of saving the vest from garage sale oblivion, I rediscover it faithfully waiting to take me on another stroll down the cherished lane we call "memory."

Most hiking trails post placards at each trailhead providing important information concerning the hiking trails. They list various things that might be encountered along the way, and how to prepare for the unexpected should it occur.

Countless calories later at trail's end, we were always tired, sore, and perhaps tending to a blister or two. Most of the time, I was wishing I had packed an additional candy bar. Even so, it was well worth it to feel that sense of accomplishment, and camaraderie; along with the privilege of sewing yet another trail patch onto my Scout vest! Wow, things seemed a lot simpler when I was eleven and twelve.

The ancient and proven life-giving path I am referencing has a trailhead, a beginning place. You will find valuable information posted there, and it begins with a word some find difficult to embrace. Yet, this word is the key to all the other information. It is the word *trust.*

When we hold tightly to trust in the Shepherd, it brings us an assurance that not only is this ancient path one to be sought and followed; but it is filled with qualities which provide a life of soundness, peace, and fulfillment.

There is no other journey like it. Unlike many other journeys found in life, this journey leaves you with no regrets!

## A Fellow Traveler

At the trailhead of this ancient path we find a man named David. He began his story as a humble shepherd, and later became a king of great influence. He was a psalmist, an anointed prophet musician writing under the inspiration of God. He penned Psalm 23, this masterpiece for the heart, unveiling the prospect of genuine peace, hope, joy and security for all of us.

David knew the stress of confrontation with wild animals, self-seeking threatening rulers, murderous attempts on his life, and the assaults of entire enemy armies. He had experienced victories against all odds, and had displayed honor, courage, and integrity throughout those battles. He knew the sorrow of falling prey to poor judgment and open sin, leading to loss, crushing personal failure and disappointment.

This great leader spent countless nights of comfort in fine palaces with the sweet aromas of fragrant oils within its confines. He enjoyed the best the land had to offer. Yet he spent many nights in dark and musty caves hiding to preserve his life from his enemies, and no doubt sharing the accommodations in the company of a cave critter or two.

The "sweet Psalmist of Israel" was familiar with evenings in open pastures, with oceans of stars filling the skies, with the experience of waking in the early morning to fresh-fallen dew and to the stirring of waking sheep.

Of all the memories from which David could create colorful and vivid illustrations of God's interaction with His children, he chose his days as a shepherd overseeing his father's sheep.

The result is a timeless pastoral song from one in passionate pursuit of His Creator's chief desires. One who has both sought and found the Lord because *he searched for Him with all his heart*.[5]

## Why a Shepherd?

David had secrets to share because he had discovered the priceless treasure of serenity by placing his life under the watchful care of the Great Shepherd of the sheep.

Isn't it interesting that God selected *a shepherd* to convey His care and interaction with us? He bypassed multiplied generations of standout chieftains, priests, rulers, and well-known personalities of many different eras. No, God represents Himself to those under His care as a humble shepherd in both the Old and the New Testaments. The Great Shepherd chose a shepherd to reveal His heart.

In First Samuel 16, we find Samuel the prophet trying to follow God's instruction to select a king for Israel from among the many sons of a man named Jesse. Samuel was initially drawn to his older sons, tall young men who seemed to be logical choices, but God corrected Samuel and turned his eyes, instead, toward David, the youngest son. God personally chose the son still in the fields, the one who was faithfully shepherding the sheep his father had placed under his care.

The Greek word used for shepherd in the New Testament is *"poimen."* It simply means "a feeder." This is one who leads sheep, feeds them, carefully watches over them, protects them, and causes them to rest and experience genuine security.

The analogy of God as a Shepherd over us goes as far back as Genesis 48:15, when, during the closing period of Jacob's life, he blessed his son Joseph. In the blessing Jacob referred to the Lord in these words:

*"May the God before whom my fathers Abraham and Isaac walked, the God who has been my shepherd all my life to this day..."*[6]

Generations later, Isaiah the prophet used the same term:

*"He [God] tends His flock like a shepherd. He gathers the lambs in His arms and carries them close to His heart. He gently leads those that have young."*[7]

And of course Jesus Himself used the analogy saying, "I am the good *Shepherd*; I know my sheep and my sheep know me just as the Father knows me and I know the Father and lay down my life for the sheep."[8]

These illustrations provide mental pictures and revelation of the security and peace Christ offers us as the Great Shepherd.

## Out to Sea

For several years in the early part of my ministry, I was asked to teach and lead worship at a senior high summer retreat for a large church in Memphis, Tennessee. The retreat was always held in Panama City, Florida, and my family looked forward to seeing the close friends we had established over time. An incident occurred during one particular summer session that is forever embedded in my memory.

The retreat center in Florida had a couple of small sailing catamarans available to anyone staying at the facilities. For those like me who are not familiar with sailing craft, this catamaran had two parallel banana-shaped hulls held together by aluminum poles. Some nylon rope, an aging sail, and a little duct tape completed the package.

I teamed up with our oldest son Joshua, who was eight or nine years old at the time, plus a camp staff person, to venture out for a sailing excursion one mid-afternoon. The wind was a bit strong and the waves were choppy, but we set out anyway.

We had no idea that just a few moments *after* we left, officials posted warning flags on the beach that high winds and rough surf were on the way. Shortly after we left, the staff person on board noticed the deteriorating weather conditions and decided we should head back to shore.

He turned the rudder, reset the sail, and had us all shift our weight to steer the catamaran back to shore, but *nothing happened*. Despite doing everything right, we were still sailing further away from the shoreline! We would later discover the problem was a broken rudder.

We tried several times to turn the little craft around, but each attempt was met with another failure. By then, the wind and waves were really beginning to build. To make matters even worse, one of the banana-shaped hulls began to take on water (they just don't make duct tape the way they used to).

We tried two or three more times to turn the small boat back to shore by building speed in the wind and then quickly shifting the sail and ourselves from one side of the catamaran to the other. All we managed to accomplish was getting ourselves farther out into the Gulf of Mexico!

I was beginning to worry because we had to hold on pretty tight when the rising waves began to break over the boat. I'm not sure how much danger we actually faced, but I was seriously concerned for my young son. My worry increased as I saw growing concern on the face of the staffer in charge of our adventure!

I prayed fervently but silently so I wouldn't reveal to Joshua just how troubled I was. Finally, we decided to try building speed and attempt a turn toward shore one more time. This time we succeeded and the boat began to move quickly toward the shore, with the sail getting a real workout under the strain of the driving wind.

Another break came as the new angle of the vessel clipped through the waves with the leaking hull now just above the surface of the water. As we hurtled toward shore, we quickly passed another small vessel coming from the opposite direction—the rescue craft commissioned to bring us back home! We continued to sail at a quick pace until we reached the safety of the shore.

As I look back on the circumstances of that day, I don't think Joshua was really concerned about the incident—in fact, he seemed energized by the quick ride to shore! For me, on the other hand, I was grateful for the moment that catamaran struck the beach.

The situation made me feel very insecure. I have asked myself since then, if I ever faced a similar situation in the future, but was somehow given my choice of vessel in advance to ride it out in, what would I choose; a raft, a catamaran, a yacht, an ocean liner, or stay on dry land?

For me, there is no question. Give me dry LAND! Forget about boats regardless of their size and stability! If a storm is coming, I'll take firm, solid, dry, and wonderfully high ground, far above the water line!

*What does this have to do with the Lord being our Shepherd?*

If you are facing the rising storm driven by the world's conflicts and challenges, would you choose to trust yourself, your personal wisdom and resources, the wisdom and resources of other men, or would you place your trust in the Lord and His infinite resources?

## Foundational

Again, there is just no contest or comparison for me. Just as dry land is the firmest physical foundation (and my personal choice) when weathering storms, so the Lord is the paramount source of security for my life.

Who is this Shepherd, the one called Lord? Which of His characteristics and qualifications would lead to such bold statements of trust?

The Great Shepherd, Jesus, is the firmest foundation you will ever find for your life. He is the Source for real hope, and the *only* one who does not disappoint. He is the ultimate refuge, the wellspring of lasting peace and joy that the world so passionately seeks. His peace and joy well up from within, because it is internal, and unaffected by outward circumstances.

In and through Him we find the quality of life sought by every human heart. He is the Lord of *all*, *everything*...really!

He knows every detail of your past, present, and future. He revealed Himself to the Biblical leader Moses saying, "I Am Who I Am." He is eternal, invincible, and able to be in all places at once! *That* is the Shepherd, the Lord of all.

Isaiah the prophet said, "To whom, then, will you compare God? What image will you compare Him to?" (Isaiah 40:18). In other words, there has never been and will never be anyone or anything great enough to compare to God. God Himself takes it over the top when He said, "To whom will you compare me?" or "Who is my equal?"[9]

James Boice wrote that God is completely "...Inexhaustible...Self-Sufficient...in need of nothing."[10] God declared about Himself, "I am God and there is no other; I am God and there is none like me. I make known the end from the beginning, from ancient times what is still to come. I say: My purpose will stand and I will do all that I please."[11]

In the Book of Acts, the Apostle Paul said, "The God who made the world and everything in it is the Lord of heaven and earth."[12] Yes, the Lord who day and night continually keeps watch over His sheep is the Shepherd. There is no surer security found anywhere outside the perfect loving care of Jesus Christ, the Great Shepherd.

Life, hope, and security come from Him, not from investments, savings accounts, positions of prominence, material possessions, or human power and control. With the "Great I Am" as our Shepherd, there should be no room in our hearts for fear or worry. "The Lord is my light and my salvation, whom shall I fear? The Lord is the stronghold of my life, of whom shall I be afraid?"[13]

Within the opening words of David's celebrated song we find the supreme revelation for hope and comfort, the foundation for enduring all of life's cares, questions, and concerns.

*The Lord who is our shepherd* is the only provision necessary. Because of Him, we "shall not be in want." He is able to shepherd, to care for and oversee, all who hear His voice and follow Him. His abilities, love, and resources are inexhaustible. With Jesus as our Shepherd, we win!

## How Does He Keep Up?

I am writing these words today as I fly to Detroit, Michigan. It is Monday and as I look through the plane window, we are descending in preparation for a landing. In full view are the tall buildings of downtown as well as surrounding suburbs and communities. I can see a flurry of activity on the ground almost everywhere I look. Traffic flows on busy streets and highways as people leave for various schools and workplaces.

Residences cover the landscape in every direction and tens of thousands of people below me are beginning their week.

How is it possible for God to keep up with everyone's life in Detroit—not to mention every other city in every other nation in the world? I don't know the how, but I do know that He *does,* and that He delights in doing so! He avails Himself to all of us, lovingly desiring to be our Shepherd if we will only allow Him to do so.

## People Watching

As I enter the main terminal, I watch hundreds of people rush and scurry to departing flight gates, checking monitors, and vying for choice seats in restaurants and coffee shops. Still others walked at a brisk pace to catch some form of ground transportation.

I found a quiet corner next to a window in the online café. Six televisions occupied the vacant nooks and crannies, all tuned to CNN News as President H.W. Bush addressed the nation.

The President attempted to address all the latest challenges stateside and abroad, including the war with Iraq, concerns for the future, and the possibility of cataclysmic terrorist attacks. Ironically, most of the patrons in the online café seemed to be indifferent to the news monitors. They focused instead on other concerns of life.

Across the café, a young man in his late twenties scanned the newspaper while sipping on a soda and dousing French fries in ketchup. He shook his head as he read, revealing his disgust or disagreement. Others talked on cell phones or typed away on laptops.

The restaurant manager appeared from behind a wall accompanied by another man with a clipboard, it's funny how clipboards subtly imply a level of authority. They came close to my table, as though I wasn't even there, and discussed how to rearrange the area to facilitate more customers.

Two Northwest Airlines workers grabbed a quick lunch while joking with a waitress. They seemed to know each other well, and I assumed they were regulars.

Across the room, a young father and his son of four entered the mysterious transit communal environment. The boy handed some used chewing gum to his dad, who in turn deftly snatched a non-sugar sweetener packet and wrapped up his son's "gift" before placing it out of sight.

As I turned and glanced through the window, a man twenty feet below me on the ground in a Northwest Airlines jacket climbed onto a mobile conveyor belt unit. When another equipment vehicle passed by, the two drivers exchanged waves and head nods, when two more workers appeared and the man greeted them as well.

I mused that he seemed to be a very friendly fellow, and wondered if he was a family man and how long he had worked there. Was he from Detroit originally? Was he always this happy—was he a Christian? I don't know.

I will probably never see that friendly baggage handler again. Nor is it likely I will ever again see those other patrons of the online café. Yet, the Great Shepherd knows them. Even in such a flood of activity, Christ Jesus was aware of each life in the café. He knew the intimate longings and needs of each person outside that airport window, and of those scattered throughout the entire Detroit terminal—and across the whole earth!

No one is beyond God's ability to care for and watch over them. Yes, it is incredible and unexplainable, but true nevertheless. He knows each life and is aware of each lifestyle down to the most minuscule of details.

His heart yearns for each of us to call to Him, to surrender to His care as the Overseer and Shepherd of our lives. He loves each of us and wants to care for us, guide us, and befriend us on our journey through this life and throughout eternity.

## A Fellow Traveler

As I sat in the café pondering my mind wandered to a friend I made on the day that, sadly, will always be referred to as "9/11." The phone rang as I left our house for the church office that morning. It was my wife, Dianna, calling from the church office. She immediately said, "Have you heard the news this morning?"

I could sense concern in her voice as I said "No." She continued, "Turn on the television before you leave the house! A plane has hit the World Trade Center!"

I quickly grabbed the remote and was viewing the live broadcast when the office phone upstairs rang. I ran up the stairs to answer the call on a portable handset and quickly returned to the living room to continue watching the live reports.

The caller said, "Brother Craig, this is Pastor Dilley Nadasen. I am calling you from the Atlanta airport, but my home is in Durban, South Africa." I tried to be as attentive as I could, but the unfolding news events of 9/11 made it very difficult.

Pastor Nadasen had been ministering in the United States and was returning to South Africa. He called to invite me to Durban to lead a worship and prayer gathering.

As we talked, I flipped back and forth between Dan Rather and Peter Jennings to take in as much information as I could. Pastor Dilley was watching CNN on the monitors in the Atlanta airport.

As we continued our conversation while watching the live reports, the unimaginable happened. A second airliner suddenly struck the other tower! Dilley asked with a tentative voice, "My brother, what is happening?" All I could say was, "I don't know." Our conversation became so fragmented in the wake of the unfolding horror that we exchanged contact information and agreed to talk later upon his return home to Africa.

Pastor Dilley had no idea he would not be leaving Atlanta that day. All commercial air traffic was grounded nationwide and Dilley would remain in Atlanta for three additional days.

Before becoming a Christian, Dilley Nadasen had practiced Hinduism as did his father and family. In fact, at one point he came close to becoming a Hindu priest, following in his father's footsteps.

He met Christ after a friend of his persuaded him to attend a Billy Graham crusade. Dilley was reluctant and almost angry when he arrived at the crusade, but the Holy Spirit had orchestrated that day so he would see and hear about the grace and gift of God.

Dilley opened his heart and received Christ as his Lord and Savior that day. He even remembers that when he walked forward during the invitation, the man who met him and prayed for him was the renowned evangelist Reinhard Bonnke!

Jesus, the Good Shepherd, the Bishop of souls, wonderfully, mysteriously, and radically changed Dilley Nadasen's life forever.

Years later on 9/11, Dilley was in the same situation I was that day in the Detroit airport. He was traveling, surrounded by people he didn't know, and waiting for his plane connection to return him home to his wife and children.

## A Song of Hope

As he sat in the Delta waiting area watching the unfolding events with passengers awaiting the same flight, some of those around him began to weep. Pastor Dilley, moved by the compassion of Jesus, rose and approached the Delta desk. He told the ticket agent, "I am a pastor. Is there anything I can do to help?"

The agent simply handed him a microphone, so Dilley began to sing "Amazing Grace" over the loudspeakers, and concluded with a prayer. He later discovered that as he sang, someone patched him into the entire Delta intercom system. His song of faith and comfort *and his prayer* were heard throughout the Delta terminal, and perhaps through the entire Atlanta airport!

Jesus the Good Shepherd ministered divine comfort to thousands of hurting and confused commuters in Atlanta on 9/11, *through Dilley Nadasen*—native of India, now a South African pastor visiting the United States. The God of all comfort ministered comfort to His own and even extended His covering and oversight to others outside of His fold.

Why? It was because of His divinely unfathomable love and compassion for people!

Delta Airlines placed Pastor Nadasen and his 392 fellow passengers in a nearby hotel during the crisis. During those three tense days in Atlanta, Dilley made himself available to those stranded travelers, becoming their temporary pastor. As he cared for and prayed with them, 70 of those people opened their hearts to the salvation of Jesus the Good Shepherd!

*"The Lord is my Shepherd I shall not want."*

He is our Safe Harbor, our Deliverer and Comforter. No other source can provide what the Great Shepherd provides. No other source has the distinction of being the Creator and sustainer of the world. We need not seek any other source because He is watching over our lives. The Bible promises us, "My God will meet all your needs according to His glorious riches in Christ Jesus."[14]

It is "The Lord" who is my shepherd. It is beyond comprehension. Jesus Christ the Lord, the Son of God, the One to whom the Father has given all authority on earth and in heaven—this is the One who is our caretaker twenty-four seven, 365. Those who belong to Him will never be in want. Why would we ever consider trusting anything or anyone else?

## Back at the Café

When I finally looked up and emerged from my thoughts, the clientele had almost completely turned over in the online café. Even the wait staff had gone through a shift change. The faces that had become familiar over the previous two hours were gone, heading off to their various destinations. New faces and mysteries occupied the tables. Even the father and his gum-loving young son had gone, but not before spilling a soft drink on their table and the floor before they left.

What little I had become familiar with in that brief amount of time had already changed. It was impossible for me to catalog so many people, so many life scenarios, so much change and activity, and so many life stories and possibilities in that one small airport café. Yet, what was impossible for me was entirely possible for the Good Shepherd.

He is forever familiar with each one of us. He knows those who are His and who know His voice. He oversees each of us, while longing to call *many more* His own.

The question is not whether there is "enough" of Him to go around, but rather, "Who will surrender and allow Him to be their Shepherd?"

"The Lord is my Shepherd I shall not want."

He is able to supply the resources and oversee all that He wants me to be and all He calls me to do. All I need to do is surrender and follow. Jesus is the Way. He is life's provision! Jesus said, "I am the bread of life. He who comes to me will *never* go hungry, and he who believes in me will *never* be thirsty."[15] It seems just too good to be true doesn't it? Nevertheless, it *is* true. God does not lie, and His *truth* brings immeasurable freedom.

As I left the café, my seat on the flight from Detroit to Memphis placed me beside a mother and her young daughter. I broke out my old composition book and began to write a few thoughts. It wasn't long before the mother, who later introduced herself as Linda, asked if I was writing for business or pleasure.

I began to share how I started a personal journal not long after becoming a Christian. She in turn began to talk about her life with her husband and children. She related how, in the past, she had attended church regularly, while her husband remained uninterested. He was totally focused on their software writing business, hoping to accumulate enough resources to comfortably retire at age forty. He was devoted to their business and his self-initiated goals, but seldom spent time with her and their two children. He was a textbook *workaholic.*

## Something Changed

This mother understandably was very concerned about the future welfare of their family. However two years ago her husband picked up a book about Christ and His church. Challenged by the book to assess and reevaluate his life, he asked Jesus Christ to come into his heart as Lord and Savior.

His life, at age 39, is now under the loving, watchful guidance of the Shepherd. Their family now enjoys a very different lifestyle and focus. This man is devoted to God, and he reads and studies the Bible and spends time with his wife and family. He hardly ever works late at the office, and he and Linda teach a class at their church. His new mission is to live in the light and liberty of a surrendered life to Jesus, the Great Shepherd.

Linda said they were recently offered $12 million dollars for their business—more than enough to accomplish her husband's old self-declared goal, but they declined the offer! They believe the Lord is using their business as a tool to minister to others. Now their life goal is Jesus, not the pursuit of wealth and self-absorbing goals. The path they are on is different now; they are covered and following Christ the Shepherd.

He is the one watching over our every move, leading our every step, caring for our every need, confronting each of the enemy's assaults, exposing the enemy's every scheme against us: He is our Shepherd.

There is no better place to invest and trust our lives, no greater security than in His hands. His "Kingdom is an everlasting Kingdom and (His) dominion endures through all generations."[16] He is the King and He is the Shepherd.

It is no accident that David the Psalmist began his glorious song of security, hope, and comfort by announcing that the Lord God Jehovah is his life's caretaker, and as a result *he will not go through life in want!* This, too, is your hope if you wisely surrender and follow the Shepherd. "The Lord will watch over your coming and going both now and forevermore."[17] Jesus is the Great Shepherd for all who will believe in Him.

We *enter* the trailhead of the Ancient Path with life's most valuable key—*trust*.

If you have chosen Christ as your covering, leader, and Shepherd, then you have nothing to fear. Life's paramount provisionary is your caregiver.

## Path Markers:

1. *Your Provisionary, your Shepherd through your life is God.*
2. *He is not overworked, He has no problem caring for you and guiding you. In fact, He wants to do it and enjoys it.*
3. *He is the Lord of heaven and earth; there is nothing He cannot do for you.*
4. *If you have wandered, relocate the Shepherd of your soul and follow Him!*

# CHAPTER TWO

# Call to Stillness

*"He makes me lie down in green pastures,*
*He leads me beside quiet waters"*

Green pastures, quiet waters. Simple and pleasant prose gently continues flowing as this spiritual tunesmith begins covering the canvas of our imaginations with hue and form. The cascading images release an array of mental depictions of serene, faraway places filled with rare beauty and warm solitude. These safe and restful hideaways, places detached from situations and scenarios of concern, stress, fear, and worry, service my heart with simplicity, contentment, and rest.

I spent most of my time at 116 North Forty-Sixth Street in Louisville, Kentucky, until I was thirteen years old. Ours was just one of many small houses with even smaller yards in that part of the city. All that separated our house from the neighbor's on both sides was a very narrow driveway and a thin patch of green grass.

None of the homes on our block had air conditioning. The only way to cool down the house before going to bed was to open every window and hope for a breeze. If all went well, the breeze came gently whispering some cooler outside air through the metal screened windows into the bedroom.

With the houses so close together, my brother and I could easily hear our neighbors talking on quiet evenings. On one side lived a family with two sons near the ages of my brother and me. At night, we could actually carry on conversations with our friends next door and never have to raise our voices! Not exactly a picture of privacy.

## Open Spaces

One of my favorite things to do as a young boy was to visit my uncle and aunt's farm in Henryville, Indiana, not far from Louisville. I would always get excited when my parents would say we were going to visit them on a Sunday afternoon because I knew it meant I would end up spending hours away from the city with its crowded houses. We were headed for the open countryside where I could roam the fields and wooded areas while the rest of the family visited with one another.

That half-hour drive to freedom seemed to be unbearably long, although I always enjoyed the portion that took us across the old K&I Railroad Bridge, which spanned the Ohio River. Its narrow northbound lane added to the adventure of the trip. I still remember the roar of the tires on the iron grid surface and the thrill of seeing the river's surface exposed right through the grid.

I could hardly wait to see my uncle and aunt's two-story home from the road. When we finally turned off the paved two-lane Indiana state highway onto their gravel drive, only a 100-yard drive up the hill to their house stood between me and freedom. It wasn't a very steep hill but when you're a boy, still in single digits age-wise, the hill seemed daunting.

Once at the top we would make a sharp left, drive under a canopy of old trees until we reached a big circular drive leading to their house. We would jump out and say hello, and then I would ask if it was all right for me to walk around the farm. As soon as I got the okay from my parents, I would head for the barnyard where all of the farm equipment was stored.

## Exploration

The main barn was always my first stop. I loved the animal stalls, the hay, the farm implements, and the two old wooden ladders leading up to the hayloft. The barnyard also featured other sheds housing a pair of old tractors just waiting for my attention.

The first was a red tractor, its pigment long faded with age, the other was a smaller gray Ford tractor, my typical target of choice for my first climb of the day after the great escape and run for discovery.

After a thorough barnyard exploration, I would climb the white board fence separating the barnyard from the extended pastures, ponds, cornfields, and timber areas. Once on top of the fence, I would jump to the ground on the other side and just stand for a couple of minutes—carefully taking in and admiring the view before descending the hillside crisscrossed with cattle paths to the lush green fields below.

I can still see it in my mind's eye. And I can easily remember the many smells that country farm contained, very different from the smells of the city. At the bottom of the hill was a large stock pond that ranked as my second stop in my journey about the farm.

A quick walk around its banks on the well-worn cattle path put me in position to watch the frogs jump in the water as I approached—without a single thought of school bells, homework, pop quizzes, or home chores. I had no worries, just fresh air, pastures, corn fields, secluded wooded areas with box turtles, rabbits, and (if I got really lucky) a small snake or two. I had an urgent appointment to skip rocks across ponds and climb overhanging limbs in a forest of big trees.

I had plenty to stir my imagination while enjoying the scenery and soaking in the peace, quiet, and simplicity. I spent hours walking around that old farm and to this day my childhood memories of my time there rank among my fondest.

What is it about a green pasture or meadow that brings such pleasure to an active mind? If you add a stream or a small pond to the mix, then you have all the ingredients necessary for a perfect time of rejuvenation.

It seems God has created us in such a way that in order to function properly, we must have both physical and spiritual resting periods, times that must be set aside to "catch our breath," if you will.

David said his good shepherd actually "made" him or caused him to "lie down in green pastures."

## What We Need

The Lord knows we need rest, and He knows *when* we need it. He knows far better than we do exactly what we need emotionally, physically, and spiritually. He knows when we are overloaded, and He will help us find rest if we will allow Him to do so. These places of rest and peace may vary in length of time, but each day requires them. The longer the trip or the more rugged the task or journey, the more rest, peace, and spiritual nourishment are required.

We need *real peace* if we have any hope of experiencing genuine rest, because rest and peace are inseparable companions. Spiritual health and rejuvenation cannot be attained if they are separated. Rest must always have peace as its cohort, otherwise, the prospect of restoration for the soul remains scant.

Unfortunately, I have learned this truth the hard way that I should never "take my troubles along" on a retreat meant to bring relief from physical exhaustion. My goal for different retreats was to find quiet rest, but all hope for rest disappeared the moment I began to dwell on some problem or conflict. Those thoughts led to concern, which produced worry (which means I *never* got the rest I needed). If you carry worry in your mind or backpack, then it won't matter that you have "retreated" to Costa Rica's most picturesque mountaintop villa overlooking the natural beauty of a secluded jungle valley. You will *still* be troubled and restless inside (and you'll have an inflated travel expense waiting for you when you get home).

I've read that sheep will only lie down and truly rest if they feel certain there are no predators or pests nearby. They need to have sufficient food, enough room so they are not overcrowded, and they have to know the shepherd is in close proximity.

Perhaps this explains why a shepherd would seek this kind of environment for his flock. Once it is found, the shepherd will then actually make the sheep lie down and rest. If the sheep do not sense peaceful safety and security, they will remain restless and edgy and will not lie down and rest.

## Zac

During his senior year in high school our oldest son pressed us to let him purchase a ball python, a snake that grows to about five feet long. This snake coils into a ball when it senses danger, thus the name, and making it a favorite of young reptile enthusiasts since it is not aggressive.

To better appreciate this story, you should know that my wife Dianna did not mind her sons having pets *as long as*: (1) they are able to live outside (unless, of course, they are hamsters) and (2) they are on the "acceptable domestic pets" list. Many people (especially moms) do *not* include reptiles—especially snakes—on *any* acceptable pet list.

Snakes are not warm and cuddly, you can't whistle for them and watch them run across the yard toward you, you can't toss them cute little colored doggie biscuits or teach them to fetch. And it is next to impossible to introduce a large snake to the "acceptable pet list" unless you find a snake that can prepare meals, perform household chores, keep its own living quarters clean, and pay a nominal rental fee. I have seen some strange reptiles on "Discovery Channel" and "Animal Planet," but they've never featured a snake with the previously stated qualities.

For reasons that remain a mystery to this day, "Zacchaeus the Ball Python" not only became our son's pet, but he even lived in Joshua's bedroom. Nothing but a mother's love for her soon-departing son can explain this phenomenon.

Joshua graduated from high school and promptly left for a short-term mission trip on Youth With A Mission's "Mercy Ships" for *several months.* That is how I became the snake's lone caretaker. Feeding time was always a challenge for me because "Zac" would only eat live food.

On one occasion, I didn't pay close enough attention, and Zac mistook my right hand for a mouse. That was the day Zac almost learned how to fly. Once my heart rate became normal again, I gave serious thought to tossing him out of our second-story window. I calmed down, granted Zac a pardon, and was much more cautious and respectful during reptile dinner hour.

One day Zac the snake managed to push his tank cover aside just enough to slip out for a spin around the house. We were about to retire for the evening when Dianna walked upstairs, glanced at the tank and discovered it was empty. She quickly came down the stairs and declared to the rest of the household in firm fire-alarm vocal tones, "That snake is out!"

Instantly we began the search. After half an hour of strategically coordinated task force operation, the dreaded serpent was still at large "lurking somewhere in the shadows waiting to pounce upon some innocent unsuspecting prey." (Okay, so that's a little exaggerated, but Zac was still at large.)

The day was over; I was tired, sleepy, and ready to stop the reptile search for the night. I made what I thought was a reasonable conciliatory suggestion only to have it quickly rejected as completely foolish and unacceptable. I proposed we simply close the door to our bedroom. After all, we could safely assume the snake was almost certainly still upstairs and incapable of pushing our bedroom door down. We could get a good night's sleep and resume the quest for Zac the following morning.

I believe Dianna's response to me went like this, "You must be kidding! I could *never* sleep knowing that snake is slithering somewhere around the house. No, *we have to find it now!*"

With that issue settled, the search continued. Just a short time later Zac was discovered—by my wife of course. We all knew it at the same time. Our clue was the clarion scream from the second floor that reverberated throughout our humble abode.

The snake made his presence known when Dianna lifted the upstairs laundry basket in the hall closet, (an act no male member of the household had thought about).

It seems Zac had pushed it up and crawled underneath to secure a hiding place for the night. That is when she heard the distinct warning hiss Zac made whenever he was being bothered.

I dutifully retrieved the wayward snake and returned him to his tank and we all settled down for a good night's rest at last. My logic before the hiss was fatally flawed: Dianna could have never fallen asleep or enjoyed any peace *as long as what she considered dangerous* was lurking about within her domain of refuge.

## He Will Provide

We are similar to sheep when it comes to danger disturbing our sense of peace. We must be free of anything we consider or suspect to be dangerous, worrisome, or predatory to truly rest mentally and physically.

Christ assures us as His followers that He can and will provide the needed resources for rest and peace. He tells us plainly we have nothing to worry about while we are in His care: "Do not fear for I am with you." In Him and with Him we can lie down worry free.

Physical rest is essential for us to proceed day after day, and spiritual refueling is even more necessary. We must receive constant nourishment to replenish our hearts. It is vital for a healthy, whole-some, fruitful future. F.B. Meyer said:

*There is no part of our nature that cries more urgently for rest than our spiritual life. The spirit of man, like a dove cannot always be wandering with un-resting wing; it must alight. We cannot forever be traveling up the rugged mountain-pass of dif-ficulty, or traversing the burning marl of discontent. We must be able to lie down in green pastures, or to pass gently along the waters of rest.*[18]

Life seems to demand a great deal of us these days. I constantly battle to lie down and rest in the very places God has prepared and led me to. I've learned that if I don't follow His leading, if I resist His drawing and don't rest and refuel, then I soon grow too weak spiritually and physi-cally to carry on properly.

If I don't do things God's way, then I will not accomplish the very things He has called me to do. He wants us to follow His spiritual rhythm of walking and resting, of taking in before giving out.

I consistently encourage those around me, and the people I pastor, to search out the place where spiritual refreshing can be found and linger there a while. If we don't, we will discover ourselves tiring on life's journey and may face eventual spiritual bankruptcy. The life-giving promises of God are true, but they are dependent upon *us* for applica-tion. We must follow, we must abide, and we must obey.

## Let Him Lead

For many years, my ministry involved a lot of travel. I enjoyed that sea-son and am grateful for the opportunity of meeting a large number of pastors, teachers, worship leaders, missionaries, and visionaries. What an incredible team of Kingdom seekers exists in our day! One of the more frequent topics we discussed was the struggle to find time in the midst of busy schedules and ministry demands to be replenished spir-itually and physically.

For more than two years, I met with a group of pastors in our city each Monday. We laughed and prayed together, and we talked about how we could change our city for Christ. Whenever we talked about our personal time with God, one or more of us would reveal a deep struggle to get to that most important place.

Our schedules are busy and our "to do" lists never seem to end, but every believer must find those green pastures and waters of rest described by the Psalmist! *You have no choice as a child of God—seek out the place of rest with the Lord!*

You cannot give away that which you do not have yourself. The Good Shepherd is always leading and revealing those places to us. Our part is to follow and take advantage of them. With divine, perfect timing, He will provide us with green pastures and waters of rest.

He knows what we need and when we need it with far greater precision than we do ourselves. He is keenly aware of what the future holds and what is required to walk through it successfully. He is aware of our efforts of self-strength and the fatigue it quickly brings upon us.

If we are wise, we will let Him lead us to the waters of rest where He will replenish and restore us. We cannot continue our non-stop pace of life without giving out physically and spiritually and eventually coming face-to-face with burnout. This is not God's way, nor is it His will!

## Seasons of Rest

Each spring the men of our church take a float trip down the Buffalo River in Arkansas. The river begins as a stream in the Boston Mountains and covers 150 miles through beautiful, free-flowing, unbridled fun and natural beauty. It winds its way through gorgeous valleys, picture-perfect forests, lush green fields, and towering limestone cliffs and bluffs before emptying into the White River.

Each turn in the river unveils new flora in God-decorated landscapes, the perfect float trip aesthetics. Our flotilla usually consists of about 25 to 30 canoes with two guys in each canoe. The river confronts us with a constant exchange of slow, calm, clear pools of water and fast-moving rapids. Cycles of sudden energy expenditure and tense navigation around rocks, boulders, and fallen trees are interspersed with times of calm and rest as we enjoy the surrounding scenery while floating the slower, deeper pools in the river.

The white water rapids are fun, adventurous, challenging, and sometimes very wet. When operator-error strikes and maneuvering suddenly goes awry, we enjoy an occasional adrenaline rush. For me, however, some of the more enjoyable and certainly more restful portions of the trip come in the slow, deeper pools of water found all along the river, especially when we move into the afternoon hours.

A recent float trip contained a real "Ozark Moment" (as one of my friends would define it). My canoe buddy, Dwayne, and I had paddled since the cool of the morning. It had been a great day, with a lot of fellowship, conversation, and laughs from guys as they passed us or we passed them.

We always gather at one particular bank on a certain bend in the river to regroup and have lunch together. On this trip, some of the guys hiked a trail leading to a waterfall after lunch. Some dove off the cliffs and swam bravely in the cool early spring water. Others just lay back on the pebbled beach, pulled a cap over their eyes and napped in the warm sun (my personal choice).

After a while, we began to nudge the canoes off the bank and return to the adventure of the river once again. Later in the afternoon, we came upon several long pools of slow drifting river. The warmth from the sun and the soft blowing breeze made for a perfect afternoon. Small colorful perch were darting about in the pristine water. Cottonwood, oak, and river birch trees dressed one side of the riverbank, and tall limestone bluffs adorned the opposite side.

At the base of the bluff lay several huge boulders completely shaded by the height and angle of the cliffs. Small minnows were breaking the water's surface around our canoe feeding on water insects and larvae floating on the surface. Some ferns and even small trees were growing from various crevices in the cliff's face overhanging the boulders.

As we drifted a minute, the location caught our attention and seemed to send out a beckoning call, wooing us from the middle of the river to the shade of the bluffs. A few of us paddled over to the unique sight and paused for several minutes just to allow our eyes to soak in the breathtaking surroundings.

We savored the moment and gave our arms a rest from paddling. Several in our group drifted past us. Not much conversation was exchanged, just a head nod, a hand wave, or a short sentence like, "Man, this is great!" Eventually someone said, "Well…" with a slight sigh, which was understood by all to mean, "We have rested here long enough, we have regained some strength and absorbed the beauty of this spot, now it's time to rejoin the rest of the group."

It was time to forge ahead to whatever adventure lay around the next bend in the river. In fact, now that we had taken a break, we were actually ready and anxiously anticipating the next adrenaline rush of rapids.

Can you see the parallel? We cannot continue in unending cycles of activity in life any more than we could canoe all day on the Buffalo River in non-stop rushing rapids. There must be some seasons of rest.

Before batteries and digital technology appeared, all watches were spring operated and needed winding. F.B. Meyer said, "There must be pauses and parenthesis in all our lives. The hand cannot forever be plying its toils...work without rest is like over-winding a watch."[19] The main spring will snap and the watch will no longer function.

The Lord our Shepherd is strong and mighty, needs nothing, and is completely self-sufficient. He created us, made a way to redeem us, and offered to lead us through all of life.

He knows every twist and turn we will confront. He knows just what is required to walk us through it. He leads us to the place of rest, and it is perfect rest! In fact, if we will follow His leading, our heart and spirit can remain in that place regardless of the activity surrounding us.

He calls to us, "Come, and lie down in green pastures, beside the still, quiet waters of rest. Yes, this is it, the place I have found and prepared just for you. Free from danger and disturbance. I am familiar with this place. I control it, trust Me, abide in Me, and abide with Me. You will need the rest for tomorrow's journey."

## We Don't Know What's Coming

I recently glanced at our local newspaper, which reported the abundance of methamphetamine use in our area. A second report described a massacre in Africa's Ivory Coast by rebels who had killed innocent women and children, and then entered hospitals and coldly butchered many as they lay in hospital beds.

Other stories noted that North Korea and Iran continued their quest for nuclear weapons, discussed the war in Iraq and warned of terrorist sleeper cells in the United States. Numerous articles described problems in Central and South America, disease epidemics, weather-related tragedies, and shaky financial markets! Let's be honest: there is not a lot of encouragement flowing from the media or much else from the world's direction to offer comfort, stability and security. The point is this: *we really don't know what is around the next bend in life.* Is it peace and prosperity or destruction, chaos, and anarchy?

Pray for peace, pray for good news, pray for God's Kingdom to come and His will to be done. Meanwhile, understand that no matter what unfolds on the world's stage, our mission as Christians remains the same until the King returns: Love God with unrestrained passion, with your whole being, and take His message across the earth.

We are not certain of all the unfolding events in life; we simply do not have the ability to forecast every detail. God our Shepherd, on the other hand, knows *exactly* what is around the next bend. He tells us not to lean on our own understanding, not to rely on our own strength and wisdom, but instead to wisely lean upon His strength and wisdom and not to fear, but to *trust in Him*! (See Proverbs 3:5-8).

He is the place of rest. His Word and His presence are the green pasture and the quiet waters your soul seeks. He is *The Way!* When He leads and makes us lie down, it is for good reason. It benefits you *and* the work to which He has called you. Use wisdom and refuse to proceed with activity again until He initiates it. Abide in Him and receive His rest and restoration.

## Overextended

During the early 1980's, I had an opportunity to set aside a few weeks from a busy schedule that involved a lot of travel. The ministry organization I worked with had entered a transition period, and its leadership decided to cease from activity for a season to search for the will of God on several issues. I was told I could pursue whatever I wanted to for a few weeks during that period.

This opened a perfect window for me to slow down, rest, and seek the Lord for my own direction as well. I wish I had used more wisdom. Instead of taking advantage of this opportunity for a sabbatical period, I opted to call some friends overseeing an international college ministry. I said I would be available to visit some of their ministries, and my call produced weeks of constant travel throughout the United States! Instead of a lighter schedule, I actually began a heavier and more rigid one.

Each day I boarded a plane, flew to a campus, ministered one night, grabbed a fitful night's sleep at a hotel, and headed to the airport to repeat the process the following day.

This went on until the night I began having trouble singing (I was a traveling recording artist and performer in those days). I brushed it off thinking it was allergy-related or perhaps the beginnings of a cold. The following night was even worse, and by the next evening I had lost my voice completely. I had to cancel the remaining leg of the tour and return home. Several days went by with no improvement. My local physician encouraged me to visit a doctor in Houston who specialized in vocal chord complications.

After a careful examination the specialist told me, "I can find no sign of disease or damage. I believe you are just over-extended. You need to rest your vocal chords."

A-h-h... back to square one. I was back to what I should have done in the first place. Did I obey the prompting, did I step through the perfectly provided window of opportunity to rest and renew? No, I pressed on telling myself the same lie you may be telling yourself at this moment: *"After all, there is so much yet to be accomplished in this world for the Kingdom."*

Though this is true, I never slowed down enough to perceive the vital importance of refueling spiritually. Nor did I understand that, perhaps, God wanted a long stretch of my undivided attention!

Although there was nothing seriously wrong with my vocal chords, it took about eleven months for my voice to return to normal. I now refer to that period in my life as my "mandatory sabbatical."

You may be tempted to struggle with my next statement, but I believe the Heavenly Father who is the fountainhead of love, provided me with no alternative except to rest. During that enforced time of sabbatical, we never missed a meal or were late paying a bill. The Shepherd provided.

The Lord, my Shepherd, *made* me lie down in green pastures. At first I was uneasy about my situation because I had no idea what my future in ministry might look like. Not only could I not sing, but for a few weeks I could only write notes and speak very softly.

It was early in this season in my life that I developed the habit of rising before sunrise to seek God. I'd get my Bible and sit quietly on our patio in the darkness until it was light enough to begin reading. That spring and summer in Garden Valley, Texas, became one of the most important seasons of my life for my spiritual growth and health. I have no doubt that God was in control of that situation-not just because of the provision but because of the true marks of God that manifested during those days.

Within the first few weeks, one clear impression came to me in the form of a question: "Am I enough?" I thought it was an odd thing for the Lord to ask. "Of course you are enough," was my response. But closer examination produced greater honesty. I discovered I was finding more of my identity in the gifting and abilities God had given me than in Christ alone.

I was far more consumed with "being successful in Christian music" than with being filled with a growing passion for the love of Christ, and His presence and Kingdom. Indeed the Lord is merciful and long-suffering, and I am still amazed that He did not just put me out to pasture at a young age in exchange for a more willing and less self-seeking vessel.

God used that time to lovingly reveal to me the many areas He would refashion and reshape in my heart. It was as if my spiritual life was a field that God continued to pass through from one side to the other, plowing up rocks and stones while continually cultivating and preparing it for His good use.

Of course, this has turned into a lifetime process rather than a one-time experience. He uses the same design and process to produce spiritual growth in all of His children. He has one goal and He will not stop until He molds us into the image of His Son Jesus.

## Potpourri

One day during that "silent" season I went into our bedroom for something and attempted to sing a few notes. When I did, my voice cracked as it had so often during those months. But this time, I actually began to weep. I don't remember much from those days, but I recall this moment vividly. Amid my tears, I asked the Lord, "Even if I never sing to anyone else, would You please restore my voice so I can sing to You in my private worship and prayer time?" Shortly after I prayed that prayer my voice began to regain its strength.

One day a friend from East Texas who had been in Christian music for years told me, "Craig, I really believe you are a little like potpourri." (I don't know any guy who wants to be compared to potpourri, but I continued to listen anyway out of respect.) "Just as the fragrance of potpourri fades over time, but the fragrance again fills the room once you stir it up—I believe that is what is going to happen to you. You feel dormant and that your gifting has faded, but as the Lord stirs you up, the gifting will return." That is exactly what unfolded in the following weeks and months. The more I sang, the stronger my voice became, and the more I began ministering again.

## Not Like Us

Sheep may not know when to rest or where to find safe places to lie down, but the shepherd knows. The one who cares for the health and safety of the sheep does whatever is best for them—*even though they may not understand his methods or timing.*

We are much the same. We forge ahead because it seems right to us, but the Lord knows every twist, turn, and steep or rugged place as well as the safe havens. He knows us better than we know ourselves. "In his heart a man plans his course but the Lord determines his steps."[20] He does what is right for us even though many times we may not understand the "whys" of a matter.

The Good Shepherd does what is best for us as His sheep. "I am the good Shepherd; I know my sheep..."[21] He not only knows who we are, but He knows what we need. When rest is required, He leads the heart to a place of refreshment; and when necessary, He makes us lie down.

It is in the times and places of His choosing that joy, peace and contentment will manifest. Just about the time you think you would like to stay in that place forever, you might hear His version of "Well...," which means you have rested and refueled long enough. It is time to move on to the next adventure around the bend in your life.

Get your calendar and block out a couple of days or so to "come apart" to quiet yourself before the Lord. If you don't come apart, then you just might "fall apart."

Find a cabin, cottage, or *any place* where you can separate yourself from distractions, schedules, and phone calls—a place where rest in the presence of the Lord awaits you. Be persistent. *You have an appointment in this place with the Great Shepherd.* Let nothing endanger or crowd out that appointment. It's there, and only there, that He will lead you and feed you in green pastures beside restful waters.

## Path Markers:

1. *Every child of God requires spiritual renewal and refreshing.*
2. *True rest is only possible when security is sensed and where peace abides.*
3. *True peace abides only with Christ, and drawing close to Christ.*
4. *He is the green pasture and still water.*
5. *We cannot fulfill His call for us without consistent periods of resting with and in Him.*
6. *Because He loves us, if necessary, He will make us lie down.*

# CHAPTER THREE

## Serenity's Fruit

*"He restores my soul"*

On Christmas Day, 2001, light sleet and freezing rain began falling in the late morning hours and continued steadily throughout the day. We spent part of the day together as a family, and planned to join friends later that day for a shared meal. It was a Christmas tradition we had enjoyed for many years, but the roads accumulated just enough ice to make us stay home, so Dianna and I spent the whole day and evening together with our three sons.

Sometime after midnight, I awoke to an extraordinarily cool house. We love the heat of our wood stove, but we always set the central heat so we'll wake up to a warm house after the fire in the wood stove burns out. On this morning, however, the furnace didn't come on; and it seemed unusually dark and quiet in the house. I noticed that the outside yard light on the utility pole wasn't illuminated.

I grabbed a flashlight and directed the light beam to the oak tree just outside the living room window. Its limbs were coated with very thick ice. It was clear the electricity was out, probably due to fallen power lines caused by the ice storm.

I put a few more logs in the wood stove and returned to bed. Some time later, I heard the wind picking up in strength, and some larger tree limbs began to crack and pop under the weight of the ice before crashing to the ground. Some of the limbs slammed into others during their fall, producing some intense noise in the blackness of the night. It was an eerie sound but I was able to go back to sleep.

Suddenly, I was startled by a loud pop followed by what was apparently a tree falling to the ground. Dianna and I quickly jumped out of bed and looked out our bedroom window with the flashlight. The entire top half of a large oak tree just twenty feet from the house had broken off before slamming to the frozen ground.

We moved to the living room and peered out window after window, seeing numerous limbs that had fallen to the ground. Dianna returned to bed but I camped out on the living room floor for a while, listening to the continual cracking and popping of the trees as more and more limbs broke and fell under the intense strain and burden of increasing ice and blowing wind.

The light of dawn exposed the extent of the damage. It was an incredible mess! We learned later that most of the region was without electricity. South of town the downed trees, snapped utility poles, and collapsed roofs made the region resemble a war zone.

We couldn't go anywhere because of fallen trees and debris blocking driveways and roadways. The first twenty-four to thirty-six hours after the ice storm seemed like an adventure. We cooked outside on a camp stove, and used candles and oil lamps to light the house at night. After that, the thrill was gone and we were more than ready for the electricity to come back on.

Day three passed, and still there was no electricity. We finally got a generator going, which brought some relief, but even that got old by day four. Finally after day five, we welcomed the wonderful hum of Benjamin Franklin's glorious discovery as it surged through the electrical lines again, restoring our cold shell of a house to normalcy.

I learned two things during what many refer to now as "The Big Ice Storm" of 2001. First, I released every romantic thought of what it would have been like to marry and raise a family during the eighteenth century. I am grateful to God for creating me "for such a time as this."

## What a Glorious Word

Secondly, I have a broader appreciation for the wonderful word, "restore." We called our local electric cooperative repeatedly during the five-day outage period, to ask when power would be restored. Each time we were told, "We are working as fast as we can, but there is just a lot of damage to repair in the area." Finally the much anticipated call arrived, "Your electricity will be *restored* shortly." I hung up the phone and said, "YES!"

Restoration! What a glorious word. Restoration means to bring something back to its former condition, to renew and reinstate. Over the years of our marriage, Dianna and I have restored antique furniture, old photos, and even houses. In ministry, we have had the privilege of seeing lives, marriages, and other relationships restored through God's grace and mercy.

You feel a sense of accomplishment and fulfillment when inanimate objects such as furniture, photos, or houses are restored. But when broken and hopeless *hearts* are restored to life again, it is impossible to adequately describe the overwhelming joy that fills your heart, regardless of what part you played in the miracle!

## Retreat

I began writing this chapter perched on top of a natural stone pillar on a cool and slightly overcast fall day in Arkansas. My chosen creative perch is located very close to Cedar Creek Canyon that drops four hundred feet from my seat, flanked on either side by sheer cliffs.

Perhaps I hadn't picked the safest place to think and write, but I couldn't resist the beckoning call of the place when I first spotted the site from a good distance down the path I was walking. I claimed that old "fieldstone pillar" as my own, and on that particular day I didn't see another person for hours—only a fence lizard and a few butterflies.

The canyon was covered with an array of trees in full fall display, including oak, pine, sycamore, hickory, and dogwood. The only sounds I heard were of the wind blowing through the trees, and the distant sound of water making its way through a narrow ravine and rushing over a cliff for the 95-foot plunge into a large clear pool of water surrounded by huge boulders at the bottom of the canyon.

To help me avoid the temptation of constantly checking the time, I intentionally left my watch in the cabin. My purpose was simple: to spend seventy-two hours alone with Jesus, reading the Bible, praying, worshiping, and writing. In this place of solitude, I hoped to find rest, quiet, and input from my heart's life source, Jesus Christ. Ideally, I would enjoy God's creation in quiet restorative fellowship amidst His breathtaking, creative handiwork.

However, the day *before* I sat on my stone perch was quite different. I was in my office wrestling with my ever-growing "To Do" list trying to "free my mind" in preparation for the three days of solitude. Yet with the passing of each half hour my "To Do" list expanded as if on steroids.

I watched my ETD (estimated time of departure) arrive and pass by as one "fire" after another burst onto the scene demanding my personal firefighting attention.

Pressures continued to expand as my own self-imposed expectations added to my frustration level. My heart goes out to the frazzled majority who probably suffer from the same situation or "condition" I am describing on a daily basis.

I planned and *desperately hoped* to leave by noon, but reality stepped in and forced a 6:30 p.m. departure. It would have been even later, but I received unforeseen assistance from an electrical outage! For no apparent reason, the power suddenly ceased in our church building and surrounding neighborhood. We saw no evidence of storms, wind, utility workers, or large squirrels. (It must have been God.)

The staff and a few others gathered outside the office door to investigate, and I suddenly sensed a window of escape. The most liberating thought broke into my cluttered mind, "Hey, I think I will take this as a personal invitation from God to leave *right now* for my three-day prayer retreat."

Perhaps being a pastor has a few perks after all! I grabbed a few things from my desk, told the staff to carry on as I rushed to the car, drove home with a ridiculous smile on my face, and threw some gear in my little green Ford Ranger.

So there I was, perched atop a stone pillar hundreds of feet in the air overlooking the magnificent landscape of beautiful Cedar Creek Canyon Falls in Petit Jean State Park, Arkansas.

As with previous get-aways and retreats, I intended to listen carefully with spiritual ears, seeking some impression or directive from the Lord. Perhaps a word of wisdom, encouragement, or confirmation of some current prayer request would reveal itself.

It took an evening and most of the first morning for my mind to begin to calm down. As I began to meditate on the Lord and His creativity in creation was displayed all around me that morning, I began to sense His Spirit of peace move into its rightful position of prominence.

I began reading Psalm 23 and as my eyes feasted on these rich words "...*He restores my soul,*" I instantly received an impression.

The *sole purpose* of the Lord, my Shepherd, for these next three days was for me to rest, so He could restore my soul, increase my strength, calm my emotions, still my mind, renew my heart, and spiritually recalibrate me.

At one point just before my escape from the office, I had actually almost decided to cancel the retreat altogether due to the flurry of activity that day. I reasoned that "there was just too much to do." I told myself I just couldn't leave my responsibilities. After all, I was behind on the "To Do" list and it was my *duty* to catch up.

However, if I canceled or even delayed the getaway just a day or two, who knows how much I could accomplish with the added time? I even had my wife call the state park office and try to cancel the first night, but it was not possible at that point so I proceeded with the retreat, which was obviously the wise choice.

*The truth is there will always be things to do.* To think you can catch up with everything on a "To Do" list in today's culture may be legitimately construed as lingering a bit too long on the border of delirium!

If you factor into the equation the fact that you work through a "to do" list specifically so you can spend some *quality time with God*, then you may safely assume your enemy, Satan, will stir in confusion and delay hoping to derail your appointment with God if he can! Most of the time, these compulsive distractions appear to us cloaked as "good intentions" or even "responsible obligations."

## The Reality

One of my weaknesses is the sincere desire to spend time with everyone in the church. I want to be everyone's friend and personally encourage them in their walk with Christ. It wasn't really possible even in the beginning when fifty to sixty attended the church. It is absolutely impossible now that we've climbed past the 200 mark. I'm still trying to break the bad news to my heart.

Friends and mentors have helped me with this over the years. They assured me that although my heart motive was pure; my goal of being everybody's friend was simply not attainable. Even so, at any given gathering at our church I cause myself undue pressure through my undisciplined and unwise use of the dangerous phrase, "Hey, let's try and get together next week!"

I'm sincere when I say it, but repentant and overextended when the moment passes. With only the standard seven days per week available to me, I just cause disappointment, misunderstanding, and hurt feelings when I cannot deliver on my good intentions. I am doing much better these days, but in weak moments, I still paint myself into a corner.

That is what produced such stress just before my escape to my stone perch in the state park. I began to reason with myself:

> *"Just think of all the people in the church I could get with if I delayed or cancelled the getaway...just let me accomplish a few more tasks, Lord. Then I can get away with You without being distracted. You know I will be able to concentrate on You with far less distraction."*

If we open our spiritual ears, we will hear the Holy Spirit whisper, "Come away! The Father desires your company, He awaits you. Come sit before Him, He loves you. It will be you and He in a quiet place. He wants to renew your strength and restore your soul as you spend time in His presence."

We forget that God created us to worship and commune with Him. We forget that He wants rich and meaningful relationship with us. We literally exist for His glory: as Isaiah 43:7 declares, "...Everyone who is called by my name, whom I created for my glory, whom I formed and made."

The Maker of the universe, who created me for His glory, actually longs for a friendship with me. God, who spoke all life into being, allows me an audience with Him!

What was I thinking? How could I possibly imagine that there are *more important things to do* than meeting with the Creator? How could I, in my wildest and most selfishly distracted moment think there is *anything* of more value than accepting an invitation into the presence of the Holy One?

Ask yourself, "Would I pass up an audience with some powerful earthly potentate or a prestigious noble or dignitary?" The honest answer is "Probably not." Yet, when the ruling Majesty of heaven and earth asks me to spend time with Him, I actually think I have to check my calendar! Something is dangerously out of place in this picture! "Forgive me Lord, please have mercy on such foolish and fleshly wrong thinking."

The King of Kings extends to you and me a royal invitation, an invitation to enter His inner chambers where He will bring peace, joy, and life to the heart. This rich communion is the deep well for the soul's restoration.

F.B. Meyer says, "Our hearts have often tasted the sweet refreshment and holy encouragement which are found in these quiet, blessed hours spent in the Most Holy Place. We know that there is nothing which is so productive of all that makes life worth having as Communion with God."[22]

Communion with God restores the soul. We simply cannot continue without abiding in His presence. We will quickly become spiritually and physically exhausted if we are negligent in our time with God.

## Unconscious

When Benjamin, our youngest son, was about six years old, he and I enjoyed an occasional Saturday morning bike ride on the country roads near our home. Now that he is over 20, I look back and wish I had taken time for a lot more of those delightful bike rides.

On one particular Saturday, we were well into our ride, when we decided to blaze a new trail. We live in a rural area with several challenging hills for amateur riders like me. We came to one of the steeper hills and decided our goal was to build up enough speed going down one hill so we could make it to the top of the next—and *then* we'd take a break.

Off we went building up speed, and all went well until we began to climb the second hill. Soon the law of gravity began to take its toll, and though I was peddled as hard as I could in my determination to reach the top of the next hill, I just couldn't keep going.

That's when things *really* went south. In my "do or die" determination to continue and not stop, I ran completely out of breath. Benjamin had been trailing behind his whirlwind dad, but now he caught up with me and had to stop. You see, by this time I was sitting on the gravel beside the road.

I was dizzy and could feel myself beginning to pass out. I started seeing little white stars, which signaled a lack of oxygen. I said, "Benjamin, don't worry, I am just going to lie down a second and I will be fine. Dad just needs to get his breath back."

That was the last thing I remember.

When I regained consciousness, the first thing I saw was the concern in Benjamin's facial expression. I guess he had good reason. After all, his dad had passed out cold on the side of a rural road. What a picture—two bikes, a concerned young man, and an "old guy" seemingly sleeping on the gravel roadside. That's not your typical Saturday morning countryside scene.

After a quick recovery, we were up and at it again. This time, however, I exercised a little more wisdom. As I think about that lesson I have to wonder, did I learn from my fiasco on the hill?

There is nothing wrong with goals, but they need to be God's goals, done His way, in His time, and with His resources. We can be running along thinking we are taking in enough spiritual breath for a given task but then suddenly find ourselves growing spiritually faint or weak.

Are we placing our relationship with God first, in order to keep our spiritual lungs healthy? We cannot continue giving out, unless we first take in, just as the lungs must first take in oxygen before they can exhale. This rhythm of balanced exchange is needed for life in the physical body and we need the same thing in the spiritual realm. We must have consistent life-giving times when we glean and receive spiritual nourishment from God's Word and prayer before we are able to share what we have been given with someone else.

## Deprivation

In most counseling situations with Christians who are disillusioned, losing hope, or living in some form of compromise with the world, we often discover that their problems began with a basic neglect of a personal devotional life.

The source of a dilemma and the ultimate unraveling of one's spiritual life may often be traced back to the gradual abandonment of vital communion with the Father. You cannot afford to neglect your communion with God—even to a slight degree.

Several years ago I walked through a bookstore and found my eyes drawn to a beautifully framed passage of scripture from Isaiah hanging on the store wall. It now hangs in our living room wall above an old piano.

That ancient prophetic passage from Isaiah always leads me to spiritual oasis:

> *"They that wait upon the Lord will renew their strength; they will mount up with wings like eagles. They will run and not get weary; they will walk and not faint."*[23]

This word constantly reminds me that I can never accomplish the will of God by the strength of my own abilities. When I forget this truth, I soon begin to feel the effects of my neglect of His Word and prayer. Worry, strife, and exhaustion move in, and I start to feel the longing for refreshing and restoration from my Father.

His Word sheds light and gives life to the spiritually exhausted, and "the Word of the Lord is right and true".[24] There is no disillusionment or confusion when I gaze into His holy eyes, only spiritual refreshing and restoration of the soul.

Before Dianna and I were married, I remember the time we gathered with her family at her parents' home. I was not a Christian at that point in my life, and I was a little rough around the edges. Nevertheless, Dianna's parents were very kind to me and I really enjoyed being around them, especially her father.

Dianna's dad had struggled with chronic lung and heart disease for several years by the time I met him, but he was quite a character! Almost every visit to Dianna's house would include a period of time with me sitting at their kitchen table having a cup of coffee and visiting with her father.

One of those visits produced yet another "oxygen deprivation" learning opportunity for me. Dianna's dad mentioned some trees in their back yard that had some large dead limbs that needed to be cut away, noting that he was going to have someone do it for him since he was physically unable to do it himself.

I knew absolutely nothing about cutting or trimming trees, but I valiantly volunteered to do the job with a borrowed and very dull hand saw and no ladder. I managed to shimmy up the tree trunk about twenty to thirty feet and reached the first fork with a dead tree limb. Then I began to saw away.

Far below me on the ground was Dianna, her parents, and her younger siblings. My plan was to cut rigorously through the limb, impressing the audience below, and then shimmy back down the tree as a conquering lumberjack!

Unfortunately, the scene did not play out as I had scripted it in my mind.

I began sawing vigorously with the dull saw while doing my best to hide any display of physical weakening. (After all, my princess and her family were watching.)

My objective before me, I foolishly pursued my goal without stopping or even slowing down enough to catch my breath. I began breathing harder and harder through gritted teeth, determined to conquer the limb.

Suddenly, as would happen years later in the presence of my son, I began to see those twinkling little stars. It was the predictable prelude to a brief unscheduled nap resulting from a lack of oxygen.

Even on the side of a country road, this normally would not be an overly dangerous situation. In this case, however, I happened to be perched 25 feet or more above the ground in the fork of a tree.

My memory gets a bit vague here, but I do recall waking up while still in the tree, somehow leaning on a limb. The facial expressions of the audience below had now changed from approving glances to ones of concern.

So far, so bad. Then, in the distance, I heard the sound of an approaching fire truck, called and commissioned to rescue one "Mr. Lumberjack."

If your laughter has subsided, let me tell you that I was able to come down from the tree in my own strength, but I would have loved to stay perched in the tree until everyone *left* the scene. At least I could have quietly escaped the country, changed my identity, and moved to Fair Isle on Shetland Island (population 70), never to be seen again.

My dilemma was the direct result of my lack of sound judgment. I should have listened to my tiring lungs as I was pushing past my physical limitations. I should have waited for strength to be restored, and then continued. All I needed was a little rest and a little foresight to pace myself—that would have changed the story's ending. (At least Dianna's father agreed to risk his daughter with me anyway—as long as I stayed away from a career as a lumberjack.)

The same dilemma arises in my spiritual life when I do not use wisdom and follow the leading of the Lord. If I attempt to push on in my own strength, I will find myself overwhelmed and spiritually depleted.

## We Need a Fill-up

The Word of God instructs all of us to *wait upon the Lord*. By waiting on Him we are restored and find renewed strength. "Those who wait for the Lord," says Psalm 37:9 "will inherit the Land."

"Cease striving and know that He is God" (Psalm 46:10). When we strive and attempt to move forward in our own strength, we follow a sad formula that always leads to falling short of God's intended goal.

There is a principle in this process of walking with God and pursuing His goals that cannot be ignored. The principle is this:

*God's goal or goals for us are always larger than we can attain in our own strength, wisdom, and ability. Thus, we must only proceed in His strength.*

There are at least two clear objectives in God's purpose for this.

First, when we know we will never attain His goals for us in our strength and with our own resources and abilities, we will continue to seek Him and His resources for the ability to attain His prescribed goals.

Second, *the completions of God's goals are only possible because of His constant intervention and supernatural assistance.* This way, He always receives the rightful honor, thanks, appreciation, and glory for the task completed.

Henry Blackaby put it this way: "God wants to reveal Himself to a watching world. He does not call you to get involved just so people can see what you can do. He calls you to an assignment you cannot do without Him. The assignment will have God-sized dimensions."[25] We must do things God's way, not ours!

In Isaiah 55:8, God says His thoughts are not our thoughts and His ways are not our ways. He goes on in the next verse to declare His ways as "higher" than ours. The prophet declared these words to a people whose heart had grown indifferent to God and His design for them. Those words *also apply to us* whenever we declare a way for ourselves other than the way He has intended.

God can do and provide anything necessary to help us accomplish the things He has called us to do. However, He is in no way obligated to be a resource for our ideas or self-exalting visions.

The Bible says, "All things were created by Him and for Him. He is before all things and in Him all things hold together."[26] We must seek Him, hear Him, obey Him, and walk in His ways. This is the divine order leading to success and victory as He defines it.

Since we were created, called and enabled by Him, we must continue in Him for the completion of our call. There must be unbroken communion between Him and us, and we must understand we are called first to be in His presence, to love Him first. Only *then* may we proceed with our outward ministry. According to Oz Guinness:

> *"Our primary calling as followers of Christ is by Him, to Him, and for Him. First and foremost we are called to someone (God), not to something (such as motherhood, politics or teaching) or to somewhere (such as the inner city or outer Mongolia)."*[27]

*"Wait for the Lord; be strong and take heart and wait for the Lord."*[28] We are instructed by Paul the apostle to, "press on," but he is not instructing us to press on in our own strength. If we rely on our own strength we will never accomplish the goals and plans of God.

*"It was not by their sword that they won the land, nor did their arm bring them victory; it was your right hand, your arm and the light of your face, for You loved them."*[29] *"Not by might, nor by power, but by my spirit, says the Lord Almighty."*[30]

We are not able to gain salvation by our own strength. Even our best, according to the Book of Romans, still falls short. It is who God is and what He has done that causes our soul's restoration. Our salvation began with God and His resourcefulness, and we must continue living the rest of our lives the same way.

If you are spiritually tired or growing weary, then remember Jesus' words of invitation leading to restoration:

> *"Come to me, all of you who are weary and burdened, and I will give you rest. Take my yoke upon you and learn from me for I am gentle and humble in heart and you will find rest for your souls. For my yoke is easy and my burden is light."*[31]

## Path Markers:

1. *Every child of God requires periods of mental, physical, and spiritual rest.*
2. *We cannot continue in the will of God in our own strength.*
3. *Rest and restoration are necessities, drawn only from time spent in the presence of God.*
4. *We are called first to Him, all else flows from that place.*

# CHAPTER FOUR

# Ancient Paths

*"He leads me in the paths of righteousness for*
*His name's sake"*

As my wilderness escape continued in the Arkansas backwoods, I spent a couple of hours hiking a hilly but beautiful winding trail on a sunny October morning. I stopped for a few minutes to rest on top of a huge boulder a little larger than a Volkswagen Beetle, situated deep within a ravine just above Cedar Creek Falls.

It was an incredibly gorgeous place, and so peaceful I could easily have remained there for hours. Just a few feet in front of me a very narrow and old iron footbridge stretched across the creek. A breeze blew through and caused the trees to sway, their leaves shaking and brushing together as though to applaud the day.

The Word of God is true! The trees do "clap their hands!"[32] I watched as a few leaves drifted gently to the ground, and others came to rest on the water's surface. The red, orange, and bronze leaves floated effortlessly past the boulder I had made my refuge, continuing their journey downstream in the cool, gently flowing creek water.

How many others have shared the privilege of resting on that boulder, wonderfully isolated from other human contact and fortunate enough to quietly enjoy and meditate upon the splendor of God's handiwork?

Not since I was a young boy had I set out alone for a day of hiking like this. A real hiking enthusiast wouldn't have considered it much of a challenge, but for me it was an adventure. It was a break from normality, a physically and spiritually rejuvenating experience.

## WARNING!!!

Earlier that day, before I discovered my secret place of refuge on the "Volkswagen boulder," I hiked further up the ravine along the canyon's rim. I passed several signs along the marked trail that said, "Warning, very hazardous area. Entry prohibited." Some of the signs even threatened perpetrators with fines.

Now why would someone deliberately break the visual flow of such a magnificently landscaped view by posting these ugly and distracting signs? Surely this is a mistake! Why would someone ruin the organic ambience of this pristine Ozark forest? Someone should complain. Was this a rudely calculated effort to intentionally spoil the enjoyment for visitors? Or was there a good and justifiable reason for the signs?

I suppose I *could have* conducted my own inspection beyond boundaries of the sign. No one was around; and no one would have ever known had I taken a few steps off the well-marked path or ventured into the "forbidden zone." What harm could possibly come from it? Even so, I knew the signs were posted for a reason.

According to the forestry service, the forest floor is fairly fragile, but ecology isn't the primary motivation for those signs. Those signs are meant to keep visitors from wandering too close to the sheer cliff edge unawares. If they did, it was possible and even probable they would fall 300-400 feet to their deaths at the bottom of the canyon. Now, I enjoy an occasional adrenaline rush as well as the next guy, but that kind of a plunge is well beyond my coping level. So staying on the marked path is a good thing in my mind!

One of my good friends is a dentist and a leader in our church. Stan loves God and is a good husband and father. He is an ex-high school quarterback who stays in great physical shape and encourages his friends to do the same. He has a strong teaching gift with the ability to share the truths of Scripture using practical examples and principles that can be easily grasped and applied. My friend has *also* provided me with a perfect life illustration that I share with his permission.

## Stay on the Path

Several years ago, Stan attended our all-church camping weekend, a tradition that began in our church when we were only twenty or thirty people strong, and continues today as an annual activity.

Most people like to meander from campsite to campsite, fellow-shipping and getting to know people who have not been in the church very long and catching up with long-time friends. On this particular weekend, we were spreading out in a huge oval-shaped campground. A small paved road encircled the area with campsites located on both sides of the lane all the way around the oval, with the restroom facilities located on the north end of the campground.

One evening Stan and another good friend, David, were slowly visiting the various campsites. You should know that our church campout tradition includes consuming large quantities of coffee while walking from site to site, conversing, laughing, and meeting new people.

As Stan and David continued their stroll drinking the coffee I mentioned, the need to locate the restroom facilities began to increase as a priority. As it just so happened, they were quite a distance from the north end of the camp. They happened to be between two campsites and in an area without much light. Stan decided to step into the darkness in the midst of some trees just off the narrow road, and save himself a long trip.

He took only a few short steps into the forest when he suddenly found himself plunging downward into the darkness. After hurtling over a very steep and rocky creek-bank, Stan came to rest among several rocks some fifteen or twenty feet below!

David heard the noise when Stan fell and quickly made his way down the steep bank. He discovered Stan climbing up the bank and helped him to a nearby picnic table. Once they reached the table, Stan passed out.

Please don't attempt this next part of the story at home—but David thought Stan actually might be dying, so he applied a single strong blow to Stan's chest with his fist while simultaneously yelling Stan's name. Fortunately, Stan immediately regained consciousness rather than succumbing to the chest slam!

Although my friend had to endure an ambulance ride and an emergency room visit, we were all relieved to learn that he had suffered no serious injuries (although his chest was sore for some reason).

The next morning many of his fellow campers explored the location of his fall to mentally reconstruct the accident. Everyone was amazed that Stan was not seriously injured when we saw the rock formations and the distance he fell. If you were to ask Stan about the incident today, I'm sure he'll tell you, "Stay on the right path. It is a *good* thing." (Especially in the dark.)

God leads us on paths of righteousness for our protection, for our personal well-being, and to insure that the optimum fulfillment unfolds on life's great journey. He never leads in the righteous life just to "prevent us from having fun, experience adventure, or enjoy good things." He is the author of all good things!

## Where He Leads I Will Go

When He leads, we are assured a firm-footed life and a good future. He leads us on this path, He doesn't drive us, push us, or say, "You go first to see if there is any danger." No, the Good Shepherd always *goes before us*, and His perfectly calculated steps bring us success and victory as we follow Him. The key is to remain on the well-marked paths, and He does this for His name's sake.

When we walk through this earth life with moral victories, with powerful overcoming testimonies regardless of the circumstances facing us, the result yields rich fruit placed before the King's throne once the journey is complete. He is honored, glorified, and yes, we win also!

We are living testimonies for Him, so others can observe His hand leading and guiding us through life. Other people constantly watch and note our responses to the varied situations that arise and challenge our lives.

When we allow Him to lead, we have the security of knowing we are walking upon a specific path *constructed with our welfare in mind*. If your Shepherd leads you there, then it is the perfect path for you-one of inner joy, adventure, and fulfillment. The Good Shepherd doesn't lead you away from life's joys. No, He leads you *away from* or *safely through* life's dangers and distractions, pitfalls that would spoil the journey and steal your joy.

## We Need a Guide

Several years ago I was invited to minister in a church in Whippany, New Jersey. One afternoon, a couple in the church escorted us on a visit to New York City. Then they led us to several destinations via the famous New York subway system.

The day was enjoyable, the fellowship wonderful, and the dinner in "little Italy" was warmly memorable. The shoulder-to-shoulder crowds on Canal Street were uncomfortable but fun, the World Trade Center site was tearfully sobering, and Times Square at night was virtually indefinable.

It was a great day, but if I had tried to make the same journey *without* good guides familiar with the local territory then the potential for an "un-enjoyable trip" on the New York subway would have been a real possibility.

Yes, there is a map in each subway car, but if you are unfamiliar with the system and the neighborhoods it serves, then all it would take is one wrong exit or one wrong train at the wrong time to turn a good visit into a miserable one.

I didn't have to think much about the details; *I just trusted our guides* and enjoyed the journey. I had a similar experience when I visited the 438,000-acre Okefenokee Swamp in Georgia, which is full of free-range wildlife including herons, cranes, egrets, alligators, and black bears.

Our family was returning from Florida one summer when we stopped for a guided boat tour in that famous swamp. We piled onto a small flat-bottom boat fitted with a small engine mounted on the stern, and made our way into the marsh. I became very directionally challenged after just a few minutes of weaving through high grass and around trees. Had we been by ourselves, and my poor family would have had to depend on *me* to get us out of the wetlands and back to safety—hope would have been slim indeed.

However, we didn't need to worry because we had a guide who knew the way. He knew the area like the back of his hand, so all we did was enjoy a new and different adventure. *Having the right leader and staying on the right path is a good thing.*

## Spheres Of Influence

A particular New Testament picture describes this "leading" principle in Second Corinthians 10:13. The Apostle Paul confronts the Corinthian church with several issues and defends his ministry and spiritual authority among them. "...We do not boast of authority we do not have. Our goal is to *stay within the boundaries of God's plan* for us...."

In other words, he was within the boundary of his authority. Another translation put it this way: "We will *confine our boasting to the field God has assigned to us...*"

Boundaries, the field God has assigned, well marked paths? Sounds confining again, but it is not. God's boundaries guarantee the most productive life possible!

The commentator Matthew Henry observed that Paul's commission "...was to preach the gospel everywhere, especially among the Gentiles, and he was not confined to one place; yet he observed the direction of Providence, and the Holy Spirit, as to the particular places whither he went or where he did abide."[33]

Another writer referred to these commissioned boundaries as "spheres of influence."[34] They are spiritual provinces given by God. What an intriguing principle of ministry disbursement God has designed for us.

He has established spiritual territories for each of us to explore, conquer, and oversee. Not only do they benefit us, but most importantly, by staying within these spiritual spheres of influence, we literally bring honor to God. We each have a vast spiritual land in which we are free to roam, and He will lead us over every *spiritual square mile* of it during our earthly lives until we experience it all.

If we are obedient, courageous and wise enough to allow Him to guide us through our assigned area for His name's sake, we will live spiritually fulfilling and purposeful lives. We will continue to discover, settle, maintain, and produce fruit on every spiritual acre within our designated territory! Never boring, always challenging, and never in vain—when the last part is conquered for Christ, we depart this earth to be with Him forever.

I frustrate and endanger myself (and perhaps others) only when I foolishly venture beyond His marked boundaries for me, cease from following His lead, or stray from His righteous paths.

Psalm 33:7 tells us that God, "gave the sea its boundaries and locked the oceans in vast reservoirs."[35] What happens when a hurricane like Katrina occurs? The water is pushed *outside its boundaries* by strong fierce winds and the results are destruction and devastation. Most of us enjoy visiting an oceanfront, but we don't like it when the oceanfront visits us.

On December 20, 1803, the United States took possession of an enormous portion of land referred to in history as the Louisiana Purchase. It was the result of much effort, struggle, and diplomacy led by President Thomas Jefferson.

This transaction extended the boundaries of the nation from the Mississippi River to the Rocky Mountains and from the Canadian border to the Gulf of Mexico. Once the transaction was complete, the land became United States soil.

Though there were a couple of boundary disputes in the beginning, for the most part it was a completed deal with 827,987 square miles of new territory for the country. Yes, there were boundaries, but within them was a vast area to begin exploring and settling.

When God instructed Joshua to cross over the Jordan into the land that He had promised Abraham, Isaac, and Jacob, the boundaries had already been determined and victory was—in God's mind—a foregone conclusion. Yet there were still enemies to confront, land to investigate, and places to settle and inhabit.

Though I can't say I fully understand it, I embrace the Lord's principle of boundaries. Boundaries exist for each of us who have been redeemed by Jesus Christ, the Great Shepherd.

As Joshua obeyed and followed God (while his understanding lagged behind), God continued to lead him on paths of righteousness. They were right paths chosen for him, good paths, paths that took him on daily journeys of trusting in the Lord.

Although God promised Joshua and the nation of Israel a land "flowing with milk and honey," they still needed to consistently seek, listen to, and trust Him. They depended on His ability and resources *daily* to uncover the treasures and enjoy the resources of their promise from the Lord.

God gave the descendants of Abraham the land because He loved them, delighted in them and made an eternal covenant with them. For their part, they sought and followed Him. Then He led and protected them for His name's sake.

In the same way, we wisely follow Him today for His honor, His glory, and His causes. It is *within His boundaries* and while *following His paths* that we find fulfillment, sweet lasting fruit for our lives, and the honoring of God.

Two other captivating passages provide insights into boundaries. The Bible says in Proverbs 22:28, "Do not move an ancient *boundary* stone or marker set up by your forefathers". To move a boundary stone was a criminal act and viewed as stealing.

We enjoy much liberty and flexibility within certain boundaries, and you and I are destined to enjoy them as we do the will of our King. However, we are *not* authorized to move or change God's boundaries simply to suit our needs or fancy. The best place to position our lives is in the *center* of what He has called us to do and in the place He has called us to be.

He has assigned us a life boundary in which to flourish and we should make it our heart's goal to love and obey Him within it. To move that boundary—or to move *outside* of His boundary—is a presumptuous declaration that we think we know more than God, and that His plan is not quite enough for us.

The temptation to test the grass "on the other side of the fence" initially seems inviting, more exciting, and perhaps to have all the trappings of a "good decision." However, like the foolish hiker who decides to bypass warnings signs and falls to his death, any decision to bypass or alter God's designated boundaries for us may result in harm.

Early in my Christian life, I would look at someone else's ministry, anointing, or realm of authority and think, "Now I just might be called to do *that*." However, *every time* I strayed from the right pathway and bypassed wisdom and restraint, I ended up in stress and confusion. Once I sobered up my thinking, relocated His boundaries for my life, and repositioned myself within God's will, then peace would return along with clarity, fulfillment, and fruitfulness.

## Fly Like An Eagle

For about three years in the early 1980's, I was the worship leader for David Wilkerson's ministry (a powerful speaker and author of several books including the classic, *The Cross and the Switchblade,* and founder of *Times Square Church* in Manhattan). Pastor Wilkerson has devoted decades to proclaiming the life and grace of Jesus.

My assignment was to attempt to bring people into a place of worship during David's ministry gatherings. On one occasion, we scheduled an outdoor outreach in New York City. During the outreach, we were to hold an outdoor event on Avenue D in Manhattan's lower east side. We were told the area was one of the worst in the nation for heroin use and drug trafficking. Early that day, workers set up a large sound system and a stage for the evening event, and for weeks before that, team members had ministered in the area in concert with local churches.

That evening the street was buzzing with people and activity. Just before we stepped out on stage to minister, one of the workers from a nearby church turned to me and said, "Except for your team members and the locals helping you, probably everyone here is either a drug dealer or drug user except for the small children."

My assignment was simple and clear: provide music to draw people to the stage so David Wilkerson could preach to them. Hundreds began gathering as the band played song after song.

Several moments later David took the stage and shared a message of God's love and mercy, but he painted a clear picture to those listening of the dangerous position they were in spiritually. He clearly described the eternal outcome if they did not change the direction of their lives. He was extremely honest and vivid, and aimed straight for their hearts.

As I listened, a very clear thought materialized in me:

*If I stood where David Wilkerson was standing and spoke the exact words he was using to address the crowd, they would either walk away or rush the stage and beat me to a pulp!*

David Wilkerson, on the other hand, was flourishing within his boundaries when he extended an invitation for people to receive Christ on that steamy hot night in July, on Manhattan's lower east side. Many came forward, most of them with tears flowing from their eyes!

This evangelist and pastor was born to do what he was doing that night. David ministered well, he soared like an eagle within his gifting and the result was changed lives and fruit for the Kingdom of God.

What would have happened if I had tried preaching and David Wilkerson decided to lead the music group? The thought sends shivers up my spine!

## The Good Way

The second passage I mentioned is Jeremiah 6:16:

*This is what the Lord says. Stand at the crossroads and look; ask for the ancient paths. Ask where the good way is and walk in it and you will find rest for your souls.*

You find the glory and rest of God along the ancient paths, the tried and true ways and paths of righteousness. Isaiah says that even in the desert there is a highway called the "Way of Holiness."[36] Once again, we are told the "paths of righteousness" are the sure and certain ways.

Boundaries, ancient markers, and ancient paths—they all sound mysterious, and so they should. After all, God is the most mysterious personality in existence!

He is absolutely the best person that could ever enter into our lives, even if we never completely understand Him or His ways. In Him is the only place the heart will ever truly be at home.

The New International Version refers to the "Way" being a "highway," which is a well- marked road designed to make travel easier. It appears that only the redeemed sons and daughters of God can use these highways, according to Isaiah 35:9.

In biblical times, only those who were ceremonially clean or pure could use certain roads or paths leading to the temple. Our God personally leads us on paths of righteousness.

Scholar and writer Edward Young said, "The way will be so clearly marked, so well constructed and so easy to follow that even fools would not go astray thereon." [37] These paths of righteousness, these ancient paths, are not constraining the liberty of the human heart and soul; quite the opposite, they free the heart and soul. When we follow them, they lead to rest.

## Where He Leads

We can find true rest, peace, security, and spiritual-centeredness only as we follow the leading of Jesus. He is the way, the truth, and the life; He is the shepherd, the bishop, the overseer of our souls, the divine strategist and shaper of all our individual destinies.

He leads us into purity and holiness, and transforms us to be as He is, and it is only through Him that the transformation becomes possible. He leads us in His way because He *is* the way. He leads us in all truth because He *is* truth. He leads us to life because He is life itself. He allows us, encourages us, and uses us to reveal His grace, mercy, and love to everyone within our boundaries.

He leads me! God leads me! My Guide is no man burdened with glaring imperfections; He is God, perfect and all-powerful! He leads me in the paths of righteousness, carefully shielding me from the enemy's countless snares and pitfalls.

Psalms 119:32 paints a beautiful word picture of life on the ancient path: "I run in the path of your commands for you have set my heart free". We can run with confidence and freedom in the path of His commands because of the leading, protection, and provision of our Shepherd.

Where do you begin? How do you find this highway, this ancient path of God? You can find The Way in only one place, a place where all of the secrets of God's Kingdom and the keys of life reside, and that place is the Bible: "Thy word is a lamp to my feet and a light to my path."[38] Within God's Word are the clearly marked paths for all to find and follow.

This may or may not sound familiar to you, but my wife says she doesn't think men are very good at finding things. Unfortunately, my track record has produced mountains of evidence to support her hypothesis. If I have trouble finding a certain shirt or some slacks while rushing to make a meeting or keep an appointment at the church, then I'm finally forced to the moment of truth, the question I always dread asking (along with most red-blooded American, European, Hispanic, African, and Asian husbands)...

*"Honey, I have looked everywhere, have you seen...?"*

The next scene is as predictable as an old Western movie plot. My wife then walks into my side of the closet and casually finds whatever I was looking for—and she does it right away. Most of the time, she makes it clear that she discovered the "lost or misplaced article" neatly hanging in the place I just passed over.

## Could You Help Me Find...

In a similar way, you sometimes feel distanced from God or off the right path in your spiritual life. You may feel hopeless and helpless to find your way back to the right path. Yet, even though you may feel as though you are too far gone in the dark forests of ungodliness, you are only a prayer away from the proven paths of God. Simply return to the simple instruction of hiding God's Word in your heart, and the light will come to make the pathway clear again.

The solution is simple and straight before us. The ancient paths are not hidden from those who search for them. We discover them quickly when we read God's Word and allow it to soak into our hearts. The Bible is the light that reveals the pathway of God. It is no wonder the Psalmist said, "Your Word I have treasured in my heart..."[39] It marks well the ancient paths, the path of righteousness. When we seek Him we will find him, and we will find how much He delights in leading us.

"Let me hear Your loving kindness in the morning for I trust in You. Teach me the way in which I should walk; for to you I will lift up my soul."[40] God loves to hear us call to Him as David the Psalmist did, and He promises us the same success when we follow the right path, His path.

"The steps of a man are established by the Lord; and He *delights* in his way. When he falls, he shall not be hurled headlong, because the Lord is the one who holds his hand. I have been young and now I am old, yet I have not seen the righteous forsaken or his descendants begging for bread."[41] We should rejoice, for these are God's words, God's promises, and "His word is flawless."[42]

When my sons were young, I sometimes took them on walks through the woods. I knew there were potential obstacles to fall on like rocks and roots, but I watched out for them so they would not stumble and hurt themselves.

When the terrain became too rough, I took their hands, and they would forge onward showing little concern because they *knew* I would not let them fall. They knew I was not going to let them be "hurled headlong" and be hurt. Now, if they were to break away and run ahead on their own, or foolishly shear off the path; then certainly there would be the possibility of a hurtful fall, but as long as they were with me they are fine.

God's paths are the safe and secure ones, and following and remaining on them is a good thing. Not only are they safe, but they lead to fulfillment and wholesome adventure.

## Path Markers:

1. *There are proven paths, which will lead us through life successfully.*
2. *God establishes boundaries for us, not to constrain us, but rather to allow us the optimum fruit and fulfillment.*
3. *His paths are the ancient paths that lead to life.*

# CHAPTER FIVE

## Valley of Shadows

*"Even though I walk through the valley of the shadow of death,*
*I will fear no evil, for you are with me"*

"Weary." I think that word would best describe the dominant facial expression among the travelers awaiting departure at the crowded commuter gate in the Memphis airport the evening I joined them. People were reading, talking on cell phones or text-messaging, talking causally with travel companions, or just starring off into space.

Nothing out of the ordinary had happened at this point on that travel day. Then a young child broke through the normality with an intensely loud voice, "Mommy, I want to go home!"

Nearly everyone within hearing range turned in his direction for a moment, and things got pretty silent. After a few seconds people resumed their activities, possibly sharing the same sentiment voiced by our tired little traveling companion. There were dozens of travel-fatigued people ready to reach their final destinations.

My wife and I had been in Louisville, Kentucky, for an unplanned three-day visit. I was headed for home (as soon as the flight arrived), but my wife would remain in Louisville another three days to be with her youngest sister and her three children.

The past three days had been tiring, sad and uninvited. We didn't come to Louisville for a casual visit with family, we were there because of a tragic accident. It was the kind of accident you hear about that "happens to somebody else," but for some reason, you doubt will ever happen to you.

Our journey began with a Saturday phone call from one of Dianna's older sisters. An accident had occurred, one destined to alter the course of a young family forever. As soon as Dianna hung up the phone, she immediately called me.

I was pulling into the church parking lot preparing for a special Saturday evening worship gathering. When I answered, her voice was trembling, and through tears she said her brother-in-law, Bryan, had been killed in a car accident. He was married to Dianna's youngest sister and was the father of their three children.

On the day of the accident, Bryan's wife Kim heard a knock at the front door of their home at mid-day on what had been a typical Saturday. When she opened the door, two men were waiting—a police officer and a police chaplain. With solemn faces and tones of deep regret, they told her the events leading to her husband's death.

It seems Bryan had lost control of his vehicle on a sharp curve and was struck by a much larger oncoming vehicle, killing him instantly.

Is it possible for a young wife and mother to process the unthinkable in a few moments of descriptive conversation with two strangers? The answer is, of course, no. It wouldn't happen in a few moments or even a lengthy period of time.

Shock, disbelief, and instantaneous despair quickly set in, as if her high-rise building of joy and safety had just been demolished by a sudden and fatally violent implosion of explosive charges. One moment she was enjoying a relationship that appeared ready to stand for decades into the future, and in the next, her life appeared to be reduced to a heap of rubble. It seems that tragic news typically arrives unannounced and void of any courtesies to the heart.

The following days were filled with tear and uncertainty about the future, with occasional waves of a dull, indefinable mental numbness common to those suffering the sudden loss of a loved one. Many questions arose, but often without truly comforting answers.

How could this have happened? Why did this happen? What possible good could come from this? A wife needs her husband, and the children need their father—what will happen now that he is gone, and how will they get along without him?

Bryan was a good husband and father. Until that moment on the curve, it was just another average Saturday for Bryan, his family, and their friends. Suddenly though, an incident took place ushering several unwilling and unaware people into "the valley of the shadow".

I think we rarely associate mercy with death in situations like this. In fact, I usually hear the comments claiming just the opposite. "Where is God in all of this?" "Where is His mercy or power to avert tragedy?"

If I could answer those questions satisfactorily, you would be reading a best seller, but I doubt that I can. I *can* say this with confidence, however: For the pure and resolute heart, there is an underlying force working 24/7 for the good, and that force is the Great Shepherd. He is the one source from which mercy never ceases to flow, even when we can't detect it initially or by our measurement find reasonable resolve.

For everyone who was close to Bryan, the tears and questions will continue for a long time, perhaps even for a lifetime. On our second day in Louisville, during visiting hours at the funeral home, I invited my sister-in-law, Kim, to take a brief walk with me outside of the building.

We strolled a few minutes without talking much, but then she began to tell me how deeply she loved Bryan as a husband, how he was her best friend, and described his quality as a father.

Kim said, "I know God cares and I know there must be a reason for this, but I don't see it." Person after person had attempted to comfort her with words, but to no avail. I actually didn't say much to her on that brief walk. I simply told her that I knew God loved her and the children very much, and that Dianna and I were available if she needed us. Then I asked if I could pray for her.

When Kim said yes, I asked God to cover her with His love and mercy, and to please bless her with an unexplainable, inexhaustible peace. Then we joined the others inside.

On the next day during Bryan's memorial service, a song played softly as a room was full of people quietly listening, and few softly wept and sobbed in grief. My wife and I sat two rows behind her sister and her children. We watched our 12-year-old nephew turn to his mother, put his arms around her and weep. I hurt for him; I hurt for all of them. I wanted to change things for them, to remove the sorrow and loss, but I could not.

I think I understood in a small way the way Jesus felt the day he saw the friends and family of Lazarus weeping over his death. Even though Jesus knew Lazarus would soon defy death as He called him out of the tomb, and even though He knew His Father was in control and that they were all in the middle of one of God's great plans, still Jesus was "deeply moved in spirit and troubled."

## We Aren't Alone

Lazarus and those close to him had entered the "valley of the shadow" and Jesus was with them, revealing His heart of compassion each step of the journey. He is a God of deep-seated emotions. Jesus Christ is not only the Lord and Savior of humanity and King of an eternal and unshakable Kingdom, but He is our best and *true friend*.

He himself said, "You are my friends if you do what I command. I no longer call you servants...instead I have called you friends".[43] God is our friend! What an amazing truth to attempt to comprehend.

Close friendships are precious and valuable gifts to honor and cherish. Next to God and family, our friends are our greatest possessions. True friends will be there in a time of need. Your friends are the ones you want to be around to share your dearest and most treasured stories, adventures and accomplishments.

True friendships offer a place of love, refuge, and safety. It is a place where truth is shared, and affirmation and encouragement are found in ample supply, along with loving correction when needed. Yet, when the relationships are based on unconditional love and are Christ-centered, the friendship continues because of the presence of genuine trust.

Mutual joy occurs when one or both of you experience breakthrough or some other achievement in life, and when you exchange sorrow and sympathy when disappointment comes knocking.

I once read that we will perhaps have only four or five close friends during our entire life times. How amazing that Jesus chooses to call us His friend and desires such close friendship.

In the story of Lazarus, Jesus wept with His friends as they mourned the loss of a loved one. And so it was with Kim's friends and family as they sat together for hours. There were times of weeping, silence, and the occasional conversational exchange. There were even a few moments when a brief smile would break through and relieve the depths of their emotions.

While sitting with Kim and her friends, I could close my eyes and imagine Jesus sitting among us, weeping, comforting and consoling.

Could we have stepped out of the natural realm and into the supernatural, perhaps we would have heard Him saying, "I am here, and I know this is difficult for you, I am with you and I will continue to be with you."

He knows the future and we should embrace Him, trust Him with our lives and all the events that take place within them, leaning on Him and "...not (on) our own understanding".[44] He is the true and forever faithful friend.

Jesus raised Lazarus from the grave, but what about Bryan?

This is where the words "I will fear no evil" grace our story. When I first met Bryan many years ago, he was a troubled young man who did not know Christ. In recent years, however, he had surrendered his life to Jesus and was a new person as a result of his confession, repentance, and the redemptive work of grace. Bryan and Kim even hosted a small group from their church every week in their home.

Their pastor was sad as he tenderly spoke of the loss of his friend, but rejoiced in Bryan's destiny of eternity with Christ. Bryan certainly had no reason to fear evil, for the Lord was and would always be with him. Having walked through the valley of the shadow, Bryan can now say with total understanding, "Death where is your sting?"

Some difficult challenges and adjustments lie ahead for Bryan's wife and children, but this same Jesus, the Great Shepherd, full of compassion, power, and wisdom; will be with them each step of the way, for He cares for all those within His flock.

## The Valleys

There are many kinds of "shadow valleys" to pass through during life besides the final valley of the shadow of death. No matter what confronts and challenges us during this earth journey, Jesus our friend and Shepherd will lead us through each step of each valley, regardless of its depth, breadth, and hidden snares. He always knows what is ahead and what is needed to continue leading us onward. His commitment and promise to His flock is, "I will never leave you nor forsake you."[45] And when Jesus says, "Never", He really means...*never*!

This life in the flesh is so brief that the Bible compares it to a "vapor." We are here one day and then suddenly we are gone. Regardless of the duration, Jesus is with us each moment of the journey—through difficult financial times, through the times when expectations turn to disappointments, and when health fails or jobs are lost. He is with us when demotion displaces the anticipated promotion, or when a move across the country dislocates us from all that has been familiar, secure, and comfortable—leaving us only with some fond memories and a few photographs in a scrapbook. He is always with us...ALWAYS!

## Walking the Path

North central and western Arkansas contain some of the most beautiful hill and low mountain landscapes in the United States. It is host to miles of wonderful walking and hiking trails, though few of the "level ones" are of any length.

Hiking in these regions usually entails walking up and down ravines, through meadows, along ridges and cliff edges and across creeks. Some are relatively easy to walk, but there are others that are challenging and difficult to maneuver.

Sometimes you enjoy pleasant and easy walking without the need to concentrate much because the trail is simple and straight. Then you graduate to trails requiring hard work and perspiration, trying trails that bless you with shortness of breath, mosquitoes, black flies, and gnats (which seem to have a rugged sort of tenaciousness in this state).

Spiritual life on earth offers us a similar journey. Sometimes you walk an easily traveled path. At other times, the way is difficult and indefinable. However, those who have Jesus as their shepherd will never travel the journey alone. He never leaves us, and by His own testimony, He is committed to us to the end of this earthly life and beyond. "Surely I am with you always even to the very end of the age."[46] Moreover, all along the way He is interceding on our behalf.

All Christians are called to a life of prayer, but there seems to be a group within each local church uniquely fashioned for the prayer or intercession room. In our own church, we could trace much of our breakthrough in the various areas of ministry to the intercessors. They faithfully gather to worship, seek the heart of God, and cry out for His will and glory to prevail. They persistently pour out their petitions before Him, and are a vital part of our church's strategic defense and offense system.

I love it when I hear the intercessors are praying for me, because I know their hearts are to see God's Kingdom come and His will be done.

I share with them almost everything I am thinking about doing in the realm of ministry so they will cover it in prayer. What a comfort and encouragement to know they love me, stand with me, and are covering me as they intercede with the Father. Over the years, I have found myself increasingly joining their ranks! Praying with them has become one of my favorite things to do.

Even as exciting and encouraging as it is to be prayed for and to pray with these wonderful earthly intercessors, there is Another who intercedes for me and for you. And He multiplies my excitement infinitely.

## Our Advocate

The Bible says, "We do not know what we ought to pray for, but the Spirit himself *intercedes* for us...And He who searches our hearts, knows the mind of the Spirit because the Spirit *intercedes* for the saints in accordance with God's will."[47] That passage alone should blast away any hardened foundation of fear from the most timid of souls. As though that was not enough, listen to this:

> *"... Jesus lives forever, He is a permanent priesthood. Therefore He is able to save completely those who come to God through Him, because He always lives to intercede for them."*[48]

Jesus CONTINUALLY INTERCEDES FOR US? He is forever our Lord, Savior, and Friend. He is the One who desires only what is good and right for us, and who knows us better than we know ourselves. He is the One who stands at the right hand of the Father, and the One who knows the past, present and future. He is God, who is perfect in every way.

So *this is the One* who is praying perfect prayers for us...continually? Now that is assurance!

Your heart should be soaring right now because of this truth, whether you are walking along the rim of the Valley of the Shadows or deep within its most dark and treacherous cavities.

This is why there should be no fear of evil: Jesus our Shepherd is with us, and through His Spirit, He is interceding on our behalf! He will get us through the valleys; this is our promise: "He will wipe away every tear from our eyes. There will be no more death or mourning or crying or pain, for the old order of things has passed away."[49]

Several years ago, a very precious couple we know entered the well-known, yet unpopular "Valley of the Shadows." They have two children and had received exciting news of a third one on the way. However, not long after this initial news, an additional follow-up visit to the physician produced much concern.

Additional tests produced a diagnosis that brought a crushing blow to their family and friends. The new life Amber was carrying was not forming properly—the baby was anencephalic, a condition in which the brain stem does not connect to the spinal column properly. The physician recommended termination of the pregnancy, but Philip and Amber immediately responded that abortion was not an option—they set their course to trust God. In their own words, "Taking the life of the baby was God's decision not ours."

Over the next several months, Philip and Amber continued to pray for a miracle. Our church as well as many others joined them in this prayer. We never ceased praying for the unborn baby girl given the name "Chosen." We continued asking God for healing, for mercy, for a miracle.

## I Don't Know

Finally, the day of Chosen's delivery arrived. We continued to pray in the waiting room and waited for news of the birth. After the baby was born, I was summoned to the delivery room to join my wife who was already there. As I walked through the door, Amber mustered up a little smile while Philip held his newly born daughter in his arms. The miracle we had all prayed for had not manifested.

Philip turned to me with tears running down his face and said something I will never forget (nor will I forget the picture of him standing there with Chosen ever leave my memory): "I just don't understand! Why wasn't she healed?"

I cannot describe to you the contorted emotions that burst within me at that point, although I suppressed and concealed them. I wanted to answer my friend's questions with perfect consoling words from Heaven, but although I desperately grasped for a meaningful phrase of wisdom and comfort, but all that came out was, "I don't know."

A few hours later Chosen took her last breath, and her brief earthly life was over. I remember later thinking, "How can I be called to pastor and minister to people, to comfort them when I don't have any words of real substance to offer them?" I needed to come through for them, but all I could say was, "I don't know."

In the following days, weeks, and months, we continued to walk with them, love them, to cry and pray with them. With the passing of years, I watched this couple minister in certain situations with a wisdom that I could never have! It was as though their spiritual growth, what had been increasing at one pace, suddenly leaped forward into a new realm after they suffered through the painful lose of Chosen.

It was like reading a book in the normal sequential way, reading a book from chapter to chapter; but then suddenly skipping from chapter seven to chapter ten! When they passed through their "Valley of the Shadow" experience, their spiritual maturity greatly escalated.

A pastor friend in our city refers to this situation as a "spiritual quantum leap." When something occurs in life that may possibly cause doubt or prompt a turn back to our own ways, more times than not it actually causes us to attain to a new level of trust in God far more quickly and inexplicably than normal!

## I Am With You

I recently received a letter from a Christian sister in South Africa, whom my wife and I briefly met at a conference in Dallas a few years ago. She loves God dearly, and she loves to pray, to encourage people, and to dance before the Lord in worship.

She wrote that on April 7th, 2002, she and a friend drove to a pastor's house in South Africa to pray for him and his family. As they pulled into his driveway, four gunmen suddenly appeared before them. Monika and her friend stayed in the car, knowing they were in the midst of a carjacking and in serious danger.

Although Monika raised her hands to signal surrender, the gunman outside her door pulled the trigger of his pistol hitting Monika several times. Monika's friend somehow managed to flee, escaping unharmed.

Monika clearly remembers seeing the trigger pulled and the flash of gunshots, but for some unexplainable reason she did not hear them or feel the pain of the bullets as they entered her body. All she remembers is saying, "Jesus, where are you? Jesus where are you?" And she remembers thinking about the Scripture passages from Jeremiah 33:3 and Psalms 91:15 "Call to me and I will answer you...I will be with you in trouble."

The gunman asked for her keys, but in the next second suddenly turned and ran away. As she lay dying from multiple injuries to vital internal organs and blood loss, she heard the voice of the Lord say to her, "You are not dying. You still have Vernon (her small son)." Later in the hospital during a five-hour surgery, doctors told waiting family members that Monika would not live because her injuries were just too critical and the blood loss too great.

For three days, she remained unconscious in the Intensive Care Unit (ICU). Then, on the third day, she regained consciousness as the impossible become possible! She remained in the hospital another 11 days before her physicians released her. One of the things they told her was that she would require at least a year of bed rest before total recovery would occur. Yet in only three weeks Monika was dancing before the Lord in worship again.

Monika knows what a "Valley of the Shadow" experience is like. She knows what it is to have the Lord, her Shepherd, walk with her each step of the way through it.

We will all walk through this valley at some point, but if we have trusted Jesus with our life and destiny, the promise is that we will never walk through it alone. This is not the promise of a mere man, but of God Himself, the perfect promise keeper. We have the assurance of His constant presence, and that is the "divine weapon" that "de-fangs" the fear of evil.

The Lord stands vigilantly by your side saying, "Call upon me and I will answer. I will be with you always!" As a pastor, it is not my role to have all the answers, nor is it yours. Our job is to point people to the Great Shepherd of the Sheep, in whom we can fully trust to always do the right thing, and who will always be there with us.

He is the Comforter, our source for genuine hope, the light that penetrates what may appear to be irreversible darkness. He is the one who will be with us always, even when we discover ourselves in the Valley of the Shadows. He simply will not abandon us, nor cower no matter how bleak the situation or difficult the challenge.

## Selchun's Story

In 1992, a mob of fanatical Muslims set out on a violent rampage against Christians living in and around the region of Kaduna, Nigeria. They burned churches and brutally attacked men, women and children.

In the midst of this cold-hearted and barbaric savagery, hundreds lost their lives because of their faith in Jesus Christ. Yet, we've learned of a brief but powerful story about a pastor whose name we know only as "Selchun." He and his wife and family loved God and shared a call to proclaim God's gift of salvation through Christ to all who would listen.

During the violence, Muslim extremists attacked Pastor Selchun and cruelly cut off his right hand. When it fell to the ground, he raised his remaining hand and began to sing these words:

> *"He is Lord, He is Lord*
> *He has risen from the dead and He is Lord*
> *Every knee shall bow and every tongue confess*
> *That Jesus Christ is Lord"*

His wife and sister listened and prayed nearby, but were helpless to intervene. That day Selchun and many others entered into the very bowels of the Valley of the Shadow.

Pastor Selchun knew the Lord was with him; he feared no evil but was able to endure and even praise God in his ordeal as horrid and inhumane atrocities were inflicted upon him by the violent and cowardly mob.[50]

*"Even though I walk through the valley of the shadow of death, I will fear no evil for You are with me..."* He will never leave us...NEVER!

## Path Markers:

1. *There is for all, an unwelcome place we will encounter, it is called the Valley of the Shadows.*
2. *If we trust in God there is no need to fear, He is in control, He is with us...always!*

# CHAPTER SIX

## Comfort

*"Your rod and your staff, they comfort me"*

When you hear the word "comfort," what images gather in your mind?

Some may picture a romantic destination such as a quiet, tiny old-world village tucked away somewhere on the shores of the Sea of Crete, or perhaps a rustic log cabin nestled in a remote valley in the Austrian Alps. Some may imagine a mountainside deep in the big timber of the Smoky Mountains. Or, you may think of a seaside cottage far off the beaten tourist's path, yet close to the township of Summerside, on Prince Edward Island (just in case you want to see a few other humans at some point).

For some, the image of comfort amounts to *any place* free from the stress and discomfort of their overcrowded lifestyle. A select few take the literal approach and think of a town just 50 miles north of San Antonio. Those who live in the area refer to it as "the Star of the Texas hill country." Its name is "Comfort" of course.

Those subjected to frequent air travel may consider comfort to be the difference between a seat in coach and a coveted seat in the first class section; where weary travelers enjoy a little better food, a little more space, and just a bit more pampering.

Perhaps you find "comfort" in the thought of that favorite chair in your living room that you can't wait to get home to and visualize as you battle bottleneck traffic on the freeway or find yourself trapped in an accident slowdown just twenty yards from the off ramp leading to your house!

For an easily pleased minority, comfort is simply an extra-thick soft cotton blanket on a cold winter's night. A few may long for a glass of cold water and a cool relaxing place to sit—after a long hot walk through sugar cane fields during a scorching day with three-digit temperatures in New Iberia, Louisiana.

Perhaps your comfort comes by avoiding embarrassment when no one was around to see you clumsily fall flat on your "south side" on the asphalt at the discount store's gas station after tripping over the fuel hose... (Yes, I confess—I was the one who touched ground zero at the gas station at 6:30 in the morning on the way to an appointment.

Sometimes comfort comes through the tune of an old familiar song that whisks your thoughts away to a warm and distant memory. To a child, it could be a hug or a word of encouragement from a favorite teacher after misspelling a word while standing before classmates.

In lonely moments, comfort comes from a friend's phone call saying, "Hey, I was just thinking about you. Are you free for coffee?"

The scenarios seem endless, but "comfort" essentially means to strengthen and give hope to another, to ease one's grief and stand alongside in times of trouble. It includes the feelings of relief, encouragement that come when you receive aid in some way.

First Lady Laura Bush said in an interview with "60 Minutes II," that when she helped plan the memorial service after 9/11, she "...wanted the Psalms and everything that was read to be comforting, because I think we were a country that needed...*comforting.*"[51]

Not long ago, I was sitting on a balcony overlooking the Gulf of Mexico and soaking in the sounds of small waves lapping the white sandy shores of the Perdido Key Gulf Island seashore. Suddenly, the high-pitched screech of a small child broke the serenity. I quickly glanced down the beach and saw a couple with a little girl who must have been under two years old.

One of the girl's parents must have stood her on the sand thinking she would enjoy the small waves washing over her feet and ankles. However, it seems the toddler was afraid of the waves, especially when placed in a sitting position. She immediately raised her arms to her mother and intensified her cry for help (simultaneously redefining the maximum level for deafening, ear-piercing sonic shrieks and stunning some confused dolphins roaming that immediate area.)

Rescue came swiftly as her mother swept the little girl into her arms and patted her on the back to comfort her and assure her that all was well. The small child locked both tiny arms firmly around her mother's neck and buried her curly head in her mother's neck and shoulder. Except for a couple of mild lingering whimpers, the crying stopped almost immediately. Why? Security was established and instantly realized. Comfort was given so sorrow and fear retreated.

## True Comfort

When God consoled His people through Isaiah, the picture He used to illustrate His compassion for them was the compassion a mother feels for her child. "As a mother comforts her child, so will I comfort you".[52] When God sets things in order - security is established, comfort comes, and sorrow and fear retreat.

F.B. Meyer says, "Whatever the Valley of the Shadow of death may stand for in our Christian experience, there is no doubt that the lonely spirit, in its passage through it, stands in urgent need of comfort." He goes on to convey the thought of there being nothing, which consoles the soul more than the words of God saying, "Comfort ye my people".[53]

All of humanity requires varying levels of comfort at one time or another. Many seek it from the world's resources, but it can never be truly found there. As with all genuine life components, *true comfort is stored in the abundant treasuries of God's heart*.

The Bible says Jehovah is the "God of all comfort." It originates from Him and He disperses it to whom and where He sees fit. The good news for us is that His heart's desire is to pour it freely into all the lives of those who will trust themselves to Him.

*USA Today* once quoted President Bush as saying, "When you realize that there is an Almighty God on whom you can rely, it provides great comfort...that's why every morning I read the Bible...."[54]

During the Christmas season of 2002, a Christian family in St Joseph, Missouri, gathered to pray for the coming year. They sought God for guidance and protection, and asked Him to unfold His plan to them for 2003. Then they began to pray for unsaved family members. The mother offered prayer for her father for whom she was very concerned. He lived on the west coast and was not a Christian, and his heart seemed cold and indifferent toward God.

As the father and mother prayed, their two children listened intently. This was the first time they had heard that their grandfather was not a Christian. When the parents concluded praying for him, the children began to pray, asking that their grandfather become a Christian and be delivered from the danger of spending eternity without Jesus.

The impact weighed heaviest on the ten-year-old daughter. She simply couldn't bear the thought of her grandfather not being in heaven with Jesus. Then a new thought entered her mind—she realized that she had never personally shared the story of Jesus with her grandfather. Perhaps he would have a change of heart if *she* told him about the gift of salvation!

As the days passed, this young girl continued to ask her parents to pray for someone to go to her grandfather and tell him about Christ. Two weeks went by after the initial family prayer time, and the family celebrated Christmas, the New Year, and even the birthday of the girl's younger sibling. Once the holidays had passed by, the reality of the grandfather's dangerous spiritual condition became even more sobering to his granddaughter.

On Tuesday morning, January 7th, at 5:00 a.m., little Sarah quietly slipped out of her pajamas, changed into some warm clothes, packed a bag, grabbed her journal and put on her warm lavender coat. She quietly slipped out of the house unnoticed and began walking. She was headed for California to tell her grandfather about Jesus.

Sometime in midmorning, after walking several miles and crossing into a different county, Sarah became tired and found a place to rest by a pond. She fell asleep for a time and when she woke, she recorded these words in her journal: *"The ground is hard, the ground is cold, but that's the way it is for us missionaries."*

Meanwhile, Sarah's alarmed parents contacted the authorities and they issued an "Amber Alert" hoping to mobilize the region and the nation to find the missing ten-year-old. Searchers eventually found Sarah walking along a road and reunited her with her family.

Sarah's journey seemed to end there amid sighs of relief and thankfulness, one that could have ended in sadness but instead ended in joy. However, the story didn't end there.

Shortly after Sarah's disappearance, her mother called Sarah's grandfather in California to alert him to the situation. When she was found safe and unharmed, the family made another call to California.

Upon hearing the good news, the man asked his daughter, "What kind of crazy idea got into Sarah's head to cause her to do something like this?" His daughter paused, and then began to tell him that Sarah had set out on her journey *with a mission in mind.*

This mother said her daughter's one mission was to tell her grandfather, whom she loved, about the love and grace of Jesus Christ.

"Dad", she wanted you to give your life to the Lord."

Silence commanded the moment, but then the uncontrollable sobs of this previously unemotional and hardened man broke the silence. At that moment, the grandfather made a decision to give his life to Jesus.[55]

To Sarah's parents, comfort came once their little girl was by their side again. In fact, that is exactly what the Greek word for comfort, "*paraklesis,*" means: "a calling to one's side."

I think Sarah experienced *comfort* throughout the entire ordeal just because God the Father loves her and her missionary heart. Her grandfather experienced comfort when he discovered the comfort of Almighty God. You only have to hear His call and come to His side.

(I must add one additional note to this miracle. I happened to be in the city of St. Joseph, Missouri, just a few days after this incident occurred. It was frigidly cold with snow on the ground—but on the day Sarah launched her mission and was exposed to the elements; the city experienced an unprecedented warm day!)

## Can Sticks Be Comfortable?

We know true comfort comes only from God, but do "the rod and staff" have to do with God's comfort?

The shepherd's rod in biblical times measured about two feet long, and sometimes featured rugged knots on one end with a thinner and smoother appearance on the opposite end. It would hang from the shepherd's sash by a leather cord and was used as a weapon for the defense of the sheep.

The shepherd's staff was about 6-to-7 feet long, was tapered at one end and did not have a crook, as typically portrayed in paintings. It was used to guide the sheep, to knock off twigs and leaves as food sources, and to help the shepherd climb steep and rocky hillsides and ravines while searching for food, water and shelter for the flock.[56] One writer said the rod had three purposes:

1.  *To count the sheep, as the shepherd would have them pass under the rod.*
2.  *To pick up their pace if they began to lag behind.*
3.  *And, to get them back into the flock if they would stray or wander off.*[57]

Phillip Keller says the rod is unmistakably God's Word:

> *"Just as for the sheep of David's day, there was comfort and consolation in seeing the rod in the shepherd's skillful hand, so in our day there is great assurance in our own hearts as we contemplate the power, veracity and potent authority vested in God's Word. For, in fact, the Scriptures are His rod. They are the extensions of His mind and will and intentions for mortal man.*[58]

Matthew Henry and other biblical commentators agree the rod and staff represent the Word of God and the Spirit of God. His rod and staff or His Word and Spirit assure me I am counted as one of His flock, that I belong to Him, and that He cares for me.

His rod and staff also bring to my attention those times I am beginning to stray, and may possibly endanger myself. If I begin to lag behind His leading, He lovingly uses His Word and Spirit to help me "pick up my pace." Finally, should I stray or wander into dangerous places, He uses them to correct and discipline me, and bring me back into the safety of the flock.

I think, *"This is great! "* when I contemplate God using His rod and staff to drive away predators, to acquire food for me, and to count me as among His flock as I pass into His place of refuge. However, I'm not so excited about their use to deliver a spiritual attitude adjustment to my backside, or to correct wrong thinking for my long-term comfort.

It is a little difficult to grasp just how all of this is supposed to increase my endorphin supply. On the other hand, I know what happens when I begin straying from God—it may eventually lead to my demise, so I should be grateful for the loving discipline of the Shepherd who will do whatever is necessary to return me to the safety of His fold.

He knows our hearts and thoughts become tainted apart from Him. It is because the Shepherd loves us that He uses His rod and staff to restore us to the place He knows is best for us.

## One Man's Realignment

Asaph was one of the leaders of David's Levitical choir, and a psalmist in his own right. He has given us a transparently honest song from his internal struggle that is relevant to nearly all of us who are committed to walking in relationship with God—and sometimes find ourselves drifting.

He opens Psalm 73 declaring God's goodness to Israel and to the pure in heart. Then he immediately launched a long confession of how close he came to slipping, simply because he could not understand how those who denied God still enjoyed all the enticements of the world, seemed to have much of the fun, and apparently received most of the "breaks" in life. Asaph even went as far as to say he envied them.

> *"They have no struggles, they are healthy...free from the burdens of common man." [59]They are prideful, violent, hardhearted and evil. They scoff, and in their pride try to crush others with their words. They even challenge God. Yet, "Look at these arrogant people enjoying a life of ease while their riches multiply."[60]*

Asaph then reflects on his own godly conduct while trying to please the Lord and to do the right thing. In an questioning moment he declares, "Was it for nothing that I kept my heart pure and kept myself from doing wrong? All I get is trouble all day long..."[61]

Have you ever felt this way? I think *most of us* would say yes. You try to be the best servant of God you can be but have a tough time locating God's blessing or favor anywhere. Meanwhile, people in the world who apparently have no desire to serve God appear to be getting along fine!

Asaph knew it was wrong to complain, but he was being candid. It is a good thing the song didn't end at that point, or Asaph might have been credited for penning the theme song for the "Order of Discontents," destined to be popular at annual self-pity conferences.

No, he went on to admit he had become confused trying to make sense of it all, and that it wasn't until he *"entered the sanctuary of God"* that all of the pieces of the puzzle finally fit together.

The Spirit of God corrected Asaph's thinking and refocused his vision away from those living in the world by the world's principles, and instead focusing upon the God of all Creation. Once corrected, Asaph was grieved at how senseless and wrong he had been. He had forgotten the all-important principle that it is not about him and this very brief earth life. He was a small part of a much larger picture, an eternal vision with the sole purpose of glorifying God.

Asaph humbly and gratefully says, "You hold me by my right hand. You guide me with Your counsel. There is nothing I want but you. You are the strength of my heart and my portion forever." [62] Then he brings the song to a stunning conclusion, as he writes, "Those who are far from you will perish...but as for me it is good to be *near God*!"[63]

The realigning process may not have been pleasant at the time, but as he once again drew himself alongside God, the reinstated comfort he found was well worth it.

## Broken

You are probably acquainted with the scripture in Hebrews that says God disciplines those He loves and exhorts them to endure "...hardships as discipline [because] God is treating [us] as sons."[64] "No discipline seems pleasant at the time, but painful. Later on however, it produces a harvest of righteousness and peace for those who have been trained by it."[65]

Like the shepherd and the sheep, God's constant care for His children includes the correcting of our unwise decisions in life placing us in harm's way.

Several times over recent years when I asked people about their relationship with their biological fathers, I have heard responses similar to this, "My father didn't care what I did growing up."

As Christians, our perfect and loving heavenly Father cares very much about the details of our lives, and He wants to be involved with us daily. When we carelessly stray onto a harmful path, He loves us so much that He will intervene to correct our course. It isn't because He lacks love for us or has a control problem, it is quite the opposite, He does these things *because* He loves us so much. Hopefully, we will understand this and be able to say as did the Psalmist "I know, O Lord, that Your decisions are fair; You disciplined me because I needed it."[66]

David was a man who loved God and was called by God for great purpose. The Lord Himself referred to David as "...a man after my own heart, who will do all my will".[67] What an honor to have the God of heaven and earth declare such a statement about a person.

However, there was a point in David's life when he let his guard down and fell into sin; and it was a hard fall. David wrote Psalm 51 sometime after he had sinned against God. In this song of confession and repentance, David cries out to the Lord and asks to once again find "joy and gladness" in his life and be restored to his former relationship with God.

In the process of writing Psalm 51, David revealed a valuable principle concerning the type of sacrifices God acknowledges and receives. Psalm 51:17 may be a difficult passage to digest at times, but it is one of my favorites:

> *"The sacrifices of God are a broken spirit;*
> *a broken and contrite heart,*
> *O God, You will not despise."*

The Hebrew word for "broken" is *shabar,* and it means to "break into pieces or reduce".[68] The word *contrite* refers to "collapsing physically." This sounds far more unpleasant to me than having a rod or staff applied to my head or back as a prelude to eventual comfort. It is very easy in difficult times of correction to wonder if God "gets some sort of enjoyment out of seeing us crushed and broken."

## Close

When my sons were young boys, anytime they could get close to the edge of a lake, river, or creek, they immediately looked for rocks and stones to throw into the water. This is part of an ancient ritual they learned from me, and that I learned from my father, who got it from my grandfather. I have a feeling this particular ritual was initiated by Adam and has continued through the male gene pool from then until now.

What happens every time a guy tosses a rock into the Buffalo River? *It sinks!* Even in the strongest of currents, the rock will resist the flow of the water and eventually come to rest on the bottom of the river.

What would happen though if we retrieved one of those rocks from the riverbed and crushed it into a fine powder of the consistency of talcum powder? The mineral content would remain in tact, but in a totally altered form. If you tossed the same stone into the Buffalo River—but in its new powdered form, it would no longer resist the flow of the river and sink to the bottom. This time it would integrate with the water and flow with the current.

How does this relate to God's rod and staff of correction? The Lord does not take joy when the hardened places in our lives are crushed and broken. However, He is pleased and joyfully receives hearts that have been altered and transformed in form by the work of His Holy Spirit. These are hearts no longer resistant or self-seeking, but conformed to the image of Jesus Christ and flowing with His will. Psalm 34:18 says, "The Lord is close to the broken-hearted; He rescues those who are crushed in spirit."

His rod and His staff (His Word and His Spirit) alter my heart when it is out of sync with His heart and will, and bent on seeking its own way. As I am conformed to His image, the resistance is dealt with and I find myself comfortably walking alongside the Father being able to say as Asaph did, "It is good to be *near God*!"

I have a fond memory of my youngest son Benjamin when he was eleven years old and attending his first week-long Boy Scout camp at Camp Pioneer. He had been excited for weeks prior to the troop's departure date, but before he left, he wanted to know if Dianna or I might be able to break away for a visit.

The troop had already been at camp for a few days before I could get there to visit a night or two. The day I arrived, I was really looking forward to seeing Benjamin. I quickly located their campsite, but I was told he wasn't there—he was busy somewhere in that 300-acre camp working at one of the many merit badge stations. I began walking the maze of trails leading from one station area to another, but could not locate him.

At one station, I discovered he now knew I was in the camp area, and *he* was going from site to site trying to find *me*.

Nearly an hour passed before we finally found each other. Once we connected, I received some great hugs, some timeless loving smiles with warm words of greeting, and the comfort of being in each other's presence. He wanted to tell me everything he had done and show me everything in the camp, and I wanted to savor every moment of it.

After a few moments, I noticed that Benjamin was not about to leave my side. He didn't even care that all of his Scout buddies were nearby; he just wanted to be with his dad.

He was experiencing a degree of security, comfort and joy by being near me. We were side by side in the mess hall, walking along the creek, in the camp Pioneer Museum, sitting around the campfire, and even as we slept in the smelly old canvas tent that night with our cots only three feet apart. There was a genuine delight in Benjamin's countenance, with deep peace, contentment and comfort. And how did I feel? My father's heart was "over the top"!

This is just a faint image of how we, as children of God, are comforted when we draw near to our heavenly Father. It is the power of His Word and the enabling ability of His Holy Spirit that draws us near to Him and causes us to remain with Him, enveloped in His presence, wonderfully protected and comforted.

> *"The gloomy ravine cannot break my courage, for all the way through I am conscious of His warm breath upon my face, of His strong grasp of my arm and of His cheery word when shadows haunt me. He knows the way, because once He trod it all alone that He might make a bridle path for me. The nights are sometimes terrible with noises, but when I look at His club, I am reassured. The torturous way is wearisome to the feet, but when I am nigh unto fainting, it is His staff that comforts me. And so I go, over the hills, down into the deep gorges, along the rocky ledges, and through the swollen streams, beguiled all the way by the song and smile of my good Guide."[69]*

## Path Markers:

1. *We all require comfort, and God is, "The God of all comfort."*
2. *His rod and staff bring us comfort, and his rod and staff are His word and His Spirit.*
3. *He uses them to encourage us, and to keep us on His path, within the safety of His flock.*
4. *He disciplines us when we are in need of it because He loves us. He does nothing which is not a direct result of His love for us.*

# CHAPTER SEVEN

## The Safe Place

*"You prepare a table for me in the presence of my enemies"*

Before you is a flawlessly prepared table, a banquet, perfectly tailored to your needs. Everything is so perfect that you begin to think it is just too good to be true. In fact, it is more than your mind, in its most creative state, could ever imagine! In fact, it is so good and perfect that you begin to wonder if the invitation was really for you, or if it was for someone else "more deserving."

Make no mistake: not only is all that you see before you actually real, but the invitation *is* for you, and *your presence* is deeply desired.

Now you are seated and no one will ask you to leave. Your emotions are in awe of this extravagance even as a feeling of being "warmly welcome" now settles in and you extend your hand for one of the delicacies on the table near you. You wonder, "*Who could be the host of such abundant provision and graciousness? Who is it who so sincerely wants me around?*"

Your host is none other than the most acclaimed, and most highly valued and renowned personality of all time. Yes, this is undoubtedly the honor of a lifetime, the paramount invitation and privilege, as you realize you sit at a table prepared for you by the Creator Himself.

Yet, with all that is at hand, there is something causing uneasiness within you, something perplexing about the scenario that brings deepening concern. You feel emotions of hesitance and even fear.

What is it? Can it possibly be? Yes! You realize that you feel uneasy because this beautiful banquet table was prepared for you *in full view of your most despicable foes*! This table is actually sitting in the very presence of your enemies! (It is very perplexing. Is this some sort of trick, a trap, or the result of some gross oversight? Can there be any rational explanation?)

David the Psalmist now moves us from the pastoral images of a shepherd and his sheep to a new scene describing himself as positioned at a table prepared by God. David is the guest and recipient of divine provision and favor. However, this table of plenty wasn't prepared in hiding far from the eyes of evil or any possibility of danger. God invited David to a banqueting table placed in the very midst of David's enemies! Quite a picture to ponder, isn't it? What possible symbolism exists here for us to uncover and draw application for our lives?

I often read this Psalm during the first few months of my new relationship with Jesus, but I just couldn't understand its meaning. However, even in my lack of understanding in those days, I *did* know that God was promising me security and victory for my life if I continued to trust the leading of the Lord.

The real puzzle was always this: why is this table, this exquisite banquet, spread out in the presence of the "bad guys"?

This illustrational transition in the Psalm marks a departure from symbolic pastoral imagery, to a more direct image relating to human activity.

> *"The image shifts in order to connect the Psalmist's message to the human audience explicitly. The image shifts, therefore, from the joys and threats of the migrating flock to the new picture of the beleaguered faithful, affirmed and honored by God in the very presence of the enemy"*[70]

## A Table

What spiritual significance or relevance can be drawn from such an inanimate object as "a table"?

I have some warm childhood memories of holidays and special times around my parents' table when we lived on the west side of Louisville, Kentucky. The family dinner table always played a very important role on Christmas Day, Thanksgiving Day, and even on the occasional Fourth of July gathering. On any of these special holidays, my mom would begin food preparations a full day in advance. It was not unusual to find her working late into the evening the day before and then again early the next morning as she continued preparations for the big event.

Before anyone could set the table, my dad would stand at one end of the table with mom at the opposite end. Together they would pull to separate the tabletop in two halves so they could insert additional "leaves" to expand the table for more guests.

Usually they invited so many family members that they had to add another table on one end of the main table, and cover it all with two or three tablecloths to create the appearance of one giant table.

Most of the time, people began to arrive by mid-morning. When the doorbell rang, Dad's role as the primary greeter would begin. From then on, the house was filled with lots of smiles, hugs, laughter and an overall air of joy.

Eventually, it was time for everyone to gather around the table and we would all take in the plethora of main courses, side dishes, garnishes and desserts spread before us. We knew it was a special occasion because of the dinnerware reserved for special meals. Once everyone was seated, voices softened until my grandfather or my dad offered a prayer of thanksgiving followed by an "Amen."

Conversations resumed, dishes were passed and the feasting unfolded along with expanding conversations about other distant family members or friends not present, with questions about school, work and hobbies. Sometimes there were reminiscent stories of past holidays and the occasional joke interspersed here and there.

That table became a memorial place, a marker where people gathered in mutual love and care for one another. We were genuinely interested in the events taking place in one another's lives. We would all tell you the food was great, but it was *the sharing of life that we remembered most of all.*

Eventually, the meal wound down and the remaining food and dishes disappeared. My mom would usually say something about how long the feast took to prepare *compared to* how quickly it was consumed... and after some stretching, came my favorite question, "Anyone ready for desert?"

In a nanosecond, I was positioned and ready for a big slice of my grandmother's homemade chocolate pie, custom made from her special recipe box.

Once desert was completed, there might be a quick walk outside, or a nap in the living room. However, it wasn't long before "the table" would beckon once again, becoming the location for competitive board games and nonstop fellowship.

Even after I grew up, married, moved away, and began a family and traditions of my own, when we returned to Louisville for a visit; where was the one place where we always shared a lot of fellowship, life and love? Right, *the table*!

After my grandmother died, my grandfather sold their home and moved in with my uncle. My grandparents had accumulated many things over their married years, too much to move into my uncle's house. Some things were dispersed among family members while others were sold.

The old dining room furniture that had been in their home for so many years and had hosted a wealth of various family gatherings was earmarked to be sold. Even though Dianna and I had no room for the furniture set, we asked if we could store the pieces some place so we could use them at some point in the future—we wanted to keep it in the family.

We had no idea what a treasure we had inherited until years later. Theses pieces of furniture are treasured for their extravagant uniqueness or superior craftsmanship. They were nice and most of it featured a zebrawood veneer surface. All I know of its origin comes from a label that is still glued to the underside of the table that reads, "The Rome Furniture Company, Rome, Georgia."

It wasn't valued because a large sum of money was paid for it. During the depression era, when my dad and uncle were young boys, they worked at Louisville's "Ideal Theater" then located on the corner of Twenty-third and Market Streets. In those days, the theater held drawings called "Bank Nights" when cash or a special prize was given away to someone who had purchased tickets to the movie.

When it was time for the drawing, my dad and uncle would bring out onto the stage an old wire drum containing the numbered ticket stubs from the crowd that evening. The manager turned the old drum, pull a stub from the barrel and then read the number aloud before the audience. Everyone watched to see the winner stand and make his or her way down the aisle, and to see or hear what they had won.

On one particular evening, a woman won the drawing and began to make her way down the aisle. Much to my dad and his brother's surprise, it was their mother! She won the dining table, buffet, sideboard, china cabinet and six chairs that night, and all for a twenty-five cent movie ticket purchase!

That event took place in 1935, and since then a lot of meals, conversations and fellowship have been shared around that dining table! Today, the amazing table sits in the dining room of our house. Now, almost 70 years later, it continues to host some very special moments. *That* is what makes it a treasure.

## Different Tables

Knowing the history of our dining room table, I'm especially curious about another table sitting against a wall in our living room. I know nothing about its history because we purchased it several years ago from an antique dealer. All we know is that it originally is from Scotland, and was built some time in the late 1700's.

For years, it was the place I would sit, read, and write in the early morning hours each day. Currently our family is creating its own tradition and history with that table, but what of its former owners?

Was it the dining table of a large family or a small one? Who were they and what were they like? Did a father or mother gather their children around that table to read a book or play games? Did the table rest in a small humble country style cottage on the edge of a meadow outside some Scottish village, or did it abide in the main room of some grand house in Edinburgh?

What were the stories shared around it? Perhaps it was used to pen letters to distant relatives, or became the favorite table of an aspiring poet or weaver of Scottish tales. The possibilities seem endless, but I can make one assumption with some measure of accuracy: I have a feeling a lot of life has been shared around it over its history.

Tables have always served mankind, and the table in David's celebrated 23rd Psalm may symbolize several things today. Tables can represent the time extreme physical activity ceases at the end of the workday, marking the transition to relaxation for mind and body.

Tremendous amounts of communication can take place between people seated at a table. It is "around a table" that countless negotiations, covenants and contracts are created and signed. Engagements, wedding plans and celebrations all occur around a table, along with the sharing and unleashing of visions, and introductions to potential new friendships as well as the celebration of existing ones.

Nations sign their treaties at tables, and tables accommodate ceremonies to honor nobility and acts of courage. You find them in mountainside castles and in small forest bungalows, awaiting practical functions as well as missions of grandeur.

Tables can represent blessing, provision, admiration, recognition, and reward as well as sincerity, closeness, and even intimacy.

B.S. Easton said, "To eat at a King's table is naturally to enjoy a position of great honor and the privilege is made by Christ typical of the highest reward. Just as my Father has granted me a Kingdom, I now grant you the right to eat and drink at my table in that Kingdom."[71]

Jesus shared some of His deepest heart-felt thoughts, revealed some of His Father's plans for redemption, and displayed His great affection for His disciples around *a table*. We call it the Last Supper. I suppose at the end of the day one could assume tables provide a pretty significant service to us after all.

F.B. Meyer said, "It is a mark of great intimacy to sit with a man at his table in the eastern (world) it is essentially so. It is not only a means of satisfying hunger, but of intimate and affectionate love."[72]

Think for a moment of someone you respect, admire or hold in high esteem. Would you consider it to be an honor if this person invited you to be a guest in his or her home and sit at their table, one especially prepared for your presence?

David says in Psalm 23 that he is seated before a table prepared for him, not by human hands, but by the creative mind and all-powerful hand of God! I know you haven't forgotten, but let us glimpse once again at the Preparer of this table. Paul the apostle discussed the identity of this Preparer and Host:

*"The God who made the world and everything in it is the Lord of heaven and earth and does not live in temples built by hands. And He is not served by human hands, as if He needed anything, because He himself gives all men life and breath and everything else. From one man He made every nation of men that they should inhabit the whole earth; and He determined the times set for them and the exact places where they should live. God did this so that men would seek Him and perhaps reach out for Him and find Him, though He is not far from us. For in Him we live and move and have our being."[73]*

Absolutely, inexplicably incredible! After reading a passage like this, it seems the only option for a child of God is to fall face down in humble adoration with thanksgiving say, "Thank You, Father, for being the most awesome force in existence and for having the capacity to love me and for wanting to have a personal, intimate relationship with me."

## The Perfect Setting

Jehovah God Himself prepared the banqueting table before David and his enemies. God our Father, perfect in every way, unlimited in power and authority, had prepared a table and a perfect banquet for us. And when He prepares a thing, nothing is omitted or forgotten, and nothing present in it will harm us.

How many times have you been seated at a table for a meal with friends or family, thinking everything needed was accounted for, and just as you bow your head for prayer or reach for your fork, someone would say, *"Oh, I forgot the such and such...."*

Just recently we sat down for dinner at home and my wife said, "Oh, I forgot the salt and pepper." My wife is fabulous, but I am somewhat convinced this is some kind of generational problem. I've heard this numerous times during our thirty-five year marriage and I've *also* heard it from mothers and grandmothers on both sides of the family!

Think about your last restaurant visit. Even there, someone at your table or next to you probably asked the waiter or waitress to bring some item that still hadn't made it to the table yet—something deemed absolutely necessary to make the meal truly complete.

When God prepares a table, however, you can rest assured nothing will be absent or in short supply. On the contrary, it will be prepared to His standard, which is *perfection.*

It is amazing to me that such perfection is prepared and delivered to David (and to us) *"in the presence"* of enemies. How can the meal and sumptuous table be enjoyed in peace while the guest is surrounded by recognized enemies?

Picture yourself seated at a table prepared especially for you by One who loves you the most, who knows exactly what you need and has unlimited resources to supply it. So far, so good.

The table is filled with so many good things that it is beyond your ability to comprehend them all. The setting is indescribably perfect and your mind fills with expectation and anticipation.

Suddenly your concentration is shattered by a familiar uneasiness as you sense the presence of something or someone evil. You feel an unsettling tingle of dread run down the back of your neck as you realize you are in an exposed and potentially vulnerable position sitting at this banqueting table. Something seems to be lurking in the shadows, something you suspect is evil intends to do you harm. Now, you are certain of it—it is your enemy!

That perfect setting has been interrupted by the imminent presence of danger. Sinister creatures linger in the dim, musty shadows, carrying concealed weapons crafted for your demise. They harbor demented, evil thoughts of your ultimate fall and destruction; waiting impatiently for an unguarded moment to strike you down. You can see that they far outnumber you and over match your ability to defend yourself.

Perhaps you can even begin to identify some of them by name: *Fear, worry, past failures, inadequacies, intimidation, anger, disappointment, injustice, unfairness and rejection....*

There are others, but even these are too many for you to retain peace of mind... your eyes have been fixed on the wrong images. There was a diversion and you were momentarily and deceptively distracted. Look across the table, set your eyes on the Host and keep them there.

Was it not He who invited you to this place and prepared this table for you? Is He not your provision in every way? Of course He is! He has prepared this table for you. His heart longs for your presence, your fellowship and for heart-to-heart exchange. His very purpose for this moment is to provide a place of rich communion between the two of you.

Do you think He is not aware of the enemy prowling about? Of course He is, but look deeply into His eyes for a moment. What do you see? There is a deep love for you, but not a single indication of concern on His part for the enemies that may occupy the shadows for now. Do you see God showing any signs of fear and nervousness? No, He doesn't even give the enemy a hint of recognition, because your host is focused on you. You are His guest.

Examine the picture again. Your enemies are hissing, frothing, and thrashing about in complete frustration. They have no choice but to stay at a distance from the table, completely out of range to harm you.

No matter how bitterly they spew venom, kick about insanely, rage at the heavens or shake their fists, they remain powerless to raise a weapon against you in this setting!

For it is God who presides over you as your Host and Guardian—you sit at *His table* prepared especially for you. There is no one like your Protector and Deliverer. He can never be overpowered, nor His authority diminished! "No one is like You O Lord; You are great and Your name is mighty in power."[74]

> *"To sit at Yahweh's table is to enjoy fellowship and communion with Him. To do so "in the presence of my enemies" is to have one's special relationship to God declared publicly in a context of divine blessing and security."*[75]

## Invitations

The church I lead is not large, yet within its people dwells a deep well of life-changing stories. Their incredible testimonies brilliantly reflect God's grace, goodness, mercy and compassion. Their situations vary in scope, but not one of their stories is any more or less miraculous than another.

Jim is a young man we met last year, and we heard his story when he began attending one of our small groups at the invitation of a friend. We watched Jim transition from attending a small group where he built friendships and learned more about what Christ had done for him, to attending the larger gathering on Sunday.

Each week his countenance continued to change as he met more people, smiled more, and began to relax around us. I could almost see the weight of the world lift from him week after week.

Jim is a carpenter, and I needed some work done at the house, so I asked him if he would be willing to do a small job for me. I did need the work done, but I really wanted to spend some time with Jim, ask a few questions, and listen. I knew he had been exposed to some situations in life that led him to be cautious about making new friends (unfortunately, this is a common occurrence).

Jim was quiet at first, but as time went on he began to talk more. What I heard was disheartening but not uncommon (though I wish it were). He came from a dysfunctional family beset with substance abuse and addiction, along with conflict and countless broken promises. He was following the same patterns until he met Jesus.

I'm fairly certain the enemy thought he had Jim so wounded, disillusioned and hardened that he would never find Christ and enter into a relationship with Him. That, however, was *another* of the enemy's miscalculations.

Jesus Christ is the fountainhead of hope, the God of reconciliation and the Healer of hearts. There is nothing He can't and will not do (within His righteous character) to clear the way for someone to choose the grace gift He offers.

As the weeks passed, Jim moved closer and closer to Jesus until one day; he surrendered his life to Him. God gave him hope and real life, and is changing his perspective. Jim is now a young man with promise and destiny.

Jim struggled with life, hope, and trust until one day he came upon a strange sight- an invitation to the table. He trusted, accepted the invitation, and now sits in the company of his Host, even though the presence of his enemies is nearby. He has learned to fix his eyes on his Host, knowing that he dwells in safety in the presence of the Lord of all the heavens and the earth.

Some time ago, we invited several people to our home for an evening of fellowship. The invitees came from different places, some of them had recently given their lives to Christ, others had renewed their commitment after years of running, and still others were in the decision-making process of deciding what Jesus meant to them.

What a great night! We just listened as folks shared about their new relationship with Christ and the paths they walked before they found Him. There was laughter, tears and thanksgiving throughout the evening as we enjoyed fellowship around the table of God's presence and protection.

Be assured, life on earth will never be perfect or wound free, not even for Christians. Life often contains discomfort and uncertainties, but in the middle of them all, we will find refuge at a table prepared for us by the King of Kings.

*"Your goodness is so great! You have stored up great blessing for those who honor you. You have done so much for those who come to you for protection, blessing them before the watching*

*world. You hide them in the shelter of Your presence safe from those who conspire against them. You shelter them in Your presence, far from accusing tongues."*[76]

## In The Midst

It certainly seems "the presence of the Lord" is where we should all seek to abide. The Bible tells us that is where we find true refuge. David declared with a thankful and overflowing heart, "You have made known to me the path of life. You fill me with joy IN YOUR PRESENCE.[77]

God's presence is not easily nor comfortably defined by human standards. His presence is mystical and supernatural, enjoying the freedom that exists beyond the halls of the realms of reason, only occasionally is it discovered skirting the shores of tangibility. Yet, trusting in Him and living in His presence is a safe harbor for the soul.

History repeatedly reveals mankind's ability to sink to unfathomable depths of depravity when it decides to live without God. Yet, even in the midst of our most evil, monstrous and demoralizing periods, people have found the power of God's all-sufficient grace, joy, refuge, hope at His table and in His presence.

On April 1, 1937, a group called the Federal Writers Project initiated a task force for a new mission. This group was commissioned by the U.S. government to locate and interview people who had formerly been subjected to slavery. The team conducted more than 2,300 personal interviews, yielding a wealth of heartbreaking but invaluable information.

Not long ago, a book was published containing several of those interviews along with some accompanying photos. One day I picked up that book and found myself staring for several minutes at a photo of a man named Wash Wilson. He was 94 years old at the time the picture was taken. He is squatting down and leaning against a red brick building in Eddy, Texas, where he lived at the time of the interview.

Mr. Wilson was dressed in black boots and rolled-up overalls with thick, wide cuffs. His right forearm rests on his knee, with a wide-brimmed light colored hat in hand. Each button on his shirt is buttoned right up to the collar. As he posed for the photo, you could see some of the pride etched on his face, along with faint remnants of a life that was neither easy nor comfortable.

Wash was born a slave in Louisiana, but his family was later sold and brought to Texas where they were forced to work and live. He described the times as a slave when, during the course of a workday, certain friends and family could be heard singing the words, "Steal away to Jesus."

To some, those words didn't mean much; but others recognized them as code words. When those words were heard in the fields and work areas, they became a message telling willing ears that a spiritual gathering would take place after dark.

Later, after the sun had set, the believers would slip off and gather at a secret place along the river bottoms out of hearing range and danger to have a church service. Their only instruments were old black kettles, pieces of iron, a cow's jawbone or a sheep's rib. Sometimes they made a drum by stretching a sheepskin or goatskin across a hollow log secured with horsehair. There, in Wash's words, they would "sing and pray all night."[78] It was there that they would find joy in the presence of the Lord, at a table He prepared for them in the presence of their enemies.

The Lord continues to enjoy setting tables for special guests. He prepares His table for you and me in the presence of our enemies, safely covered in the security of His refuge. His invitation extends to us all, the table awaits our attention and presence. Yes, the enemy may pace impatiently around the perimeter to do harm, but we are to fix our gaze upon the face of the Host, the One who prepared the table and protect us as we rest in His presence. Experience the joy that comes from being in His presence. Come and dine!

## Path Markers:

1. *God invites us to a place protected by Him.*
2. *His provision for us is perfectly designed to meet our need.*

# CHAPTER EIGHT

## Overflowing Favor

*"You anoint my head with oil, my cup overflows"*

The first riding lawnmower I owned after I married Dianna originally belonged to my grandfather. He had purchased it late in his life to cut his small yard in Louisville, so the mower was small as well. He took very good care of it, and though I did my best to keep up the tradition, that poor mower just wasn't made for the wear and tear we exposed it to.

We used it to cut a very rough and very large yard. One Saturday, I was working with the weed-eater while Dianna mowed the yard using the old riding mower. Everything stopped after I heard Dianna scream, and quickly spun around to see what had happened. The mower engine was still running but it was not moving.

Dianna, however, was doing her best to protect her head from spewing oil (it was a "gusher" actually). Something on the mower had blown and oil was shooting from the top of the engine behind the rider's seat. That stream of hot oil was shooting more than two-feet into the air and covering Dianna's head and back! Now it's a funny story today, but Dianna was not very amused the day she tried to wash hot Quaker State 10W-30 from her long curly locks!

Another oil incident I remember occurred years ago when two men approached a well-known evangelist in his office with a request. These men asked for permission to anoint him with oil and pray for his ministry. This seemed like a kind and well-intended gesture, so the evangelist consented to their request.

He closed his eyes and waited for them to pray, not knowing that the two had no intention of applying just a few drops of oil to his forehead from a little bottle of olive oil. They had bigger and better plans. As they prayed, they began to pour freely from a *quart container* they had brought along for their mission.

The evangelist was left standing with oil dripping from his head *and flowing down* onto his shirt and brown leather jacket! I wasn't present at the time, but the story and mental picture has stuck with me for years. The moral of this story may be: "when approached by oil-bearing intercessors, keep one eye open."

## My Cup Overflows

Perhaps your mind produces a similar picture when you read, *"You anoint my head with oil, my cup overflows."*

The Psalmist, however, is joyful and glad because God is anointing his head with oil. There is obviously a blessing of God to receive, but what is being communicated to us in this passage? What does the oil do and what does it represent?

First, examine the oil itself for a moment. Oils of all forms are very valuable in everyday life, as well as in the symbolism of the Bible. In life, oil keeps moving parts working. In many engines, oil is used to lubricate the moving parts and prevent friction and heat buildup, which eventually wears out engines. Oil is used to silence squeaking doors and hinges. Certain oils prevent furniture woods from drying and cracking, some are great for cooking, while other oils prevent skin damage from exposure to the sun and other harsh weather conditions.

> *"Anointing with oil originated in the eastern parts of the world, and was used to bring relief from the extreme heat of the sun. Oil or animal grease was rubbed on the body to deter some of the sun's rays. As time progressed and civilization advanced, the oils were refined and eventually enhanced perfumed oils were developed and introduced. Some oils were used for health reasons (and still are to this day)."[79]*

It was customary in the East to anoint guests with fragrant oils. It was a sign of blessing, favor, and honor as well as protection. As long as the guests remained under the care of their host, they were defended and protected by their host.

Considering the weight of this symbolism, imagine how David felt when Samuel anointed him as a future king. Surely, his heart filled with gratitude and humility as he experienced the honor and favor of God.

## The Head

More than 30 years ago, Phillip Keller, a former shepherd himself, authored a book entitled, *A Shepherd looks at Psalm 23*. He described in detail the importance of oil in caring for sheep. During the hot summer months, sheep are vulnerable to various winged parasites such as gnats, flies and mosquitoes. He described one variety of fly that so irritates sheep that when they sense it is present, they become frantic with fear and panic. Sometimes, they even attempt to run away from the pest.

When these flies are around, the sheep will begin stomping their hooves and may even run until they drop to the ground from physical exhaustion. "At the first sign of flies among the flock, (the shepherd) will apply an antidote to their heads...once the oil is applied," there is an instant behavioral change.[80] Keller said when the oil was administered to his flock, the pest was dealt with and the sheep returned to a state of peaceful tranquility almost immediately!

A couple of years ago, I took a three-day prayer retreat at a small woodlands cottage situated in the hill country bordering Northwest Arkansas and Southwest Missouri. To reach the cottage I had to drive up a very steep gravel road lined with trees, and then turned onto a level lane that ran horizontal to the hills for a couple of hundred yards.

There, nestled in the wooded hillside on the north side of the lane was a small cottage of nearly storybook proportion, dedicated by its owners and builders as a place for pilgrims to come for refuge and prayer.

After unloading a few items from my truck, this pilgrim decided to take a brief prayer-walk to get the weekend off to a right start. On the north side of the cottage was a view of valleys and rolling foothills, miles of farmland, stock ponds, and woodland areas. To the south, from the hilltop ridge, as far as my eyes could see from the east to west, stretched a clearing I thought would offer a better view, and might be a great place to sit in stillness before the Lord.

I began walking toward my goal, enjoying the rays of sunshine that managed to break through a few holes in the forest canopy. After about fifty yards, I spotted a large great horned owl perched in a tree on the low side of the hill. The owl was 20-feet or more above the ground, but because I was higher on the hillside, we were at eye level with one another. He didn't move, but his gaze never left me as I walked past him.

Now I was really getting excited. What other encounters awaited me with the area wildlife and landscape during this walk and retreat?

Suddenly, a couple of gnats appeared from seemingly nowhere to buzz around my head. *No big deal*, I thought. *After all, I am in the woods. There are any number of insects and other living creatures in these woods, and these guys are really small.*

I decided to just continue walking to the top of the ridge, and refused to be disturbed by a couple of little bugs.

Within seconds, I seemed to have stumbled into some sort of "gnat family reunion," and evidently I was the main course for dinner! I swatted and fanned my hands as fast as I could, especially around my eyes. (That seemed to be where they wanted to pitch camp for a while.)

Then it happened! One of the more aggressive militant gnat guys strategically penetrated my defense mechanism (my rapidly fanning hands) during his sortie. He successfully landed in my eye, disabling fifty percent of my vision. Now the "giant invader" was handicapped and more vulnerable to the attacks of these heartless little cannibals! That was when I resorted to a less noble emergency evasive action...I retreated in the most expeditious manner. (I ran!)

After a quick dash back to the cottage, I "anointed" myself with oil (OFF! Deep Woods®). Then I struck out once again on my mission, and this time the tiny predators remained a safe distance away and tranquility returned—all because of *"oil."*

## Spiritual Oil

Look again at David's words: "You prepare a table for me in the presence of my enemies. *You anoint my head with oil*, my cup overflows." David's enemies look on helplessly, powerless to do him harm because of God's presence and authority. Old Testament scholars, Keil and Delitzsch describe the scene this way:

> *"See how God provides bountifully for His guest, anoints him with sweet perfumes as at a joyous and magnificent banquet, ('with my own eyes I have seen the downfall of my enemies; with my own eyes I have heard the defeat of my wicked opponents' Ps. 92:11), and fills his cup to excess."*[81]

God's oil of anointing brings rich blessing and provision with peace and joy. We can and should always trust this Holy extravagant provision. God gives "...wine that gladdens the heart of man, oil to make his face shine..."[82] "The oil of gladness will be given instead of mourning."[83]

The oil is rich, its anointing gladdens the heart, but what is the oil, what does it symbolize and represent? It represents none other than the Holy Spirit. Biblical commentators unite in reference to the oil being a symbol of the Holy Spirit. "Oil typifies the refreshing and restoring ministry of the Holy Spirit."[84] It clearly represents the anointing of the Holy Spirit. Throughout the Bible, oil continues to be an important symbol of the Holy Spirit".[85]

Yes, the Lord anoints us with His oil, the Holy Spirit. Just as natural oil possesses many valuable characteristics and purposes, so does spiritual oil offer many invaluable characteristics and purposes as God anoints us with the third person of the Triune Godhead.

The Holy Spirit is referred to as the *Counselor* and *Enabler.* Jesus told His disciples in John 16:7b, "Unless I go away, the Counselor [Comforter] will not come to you; but if I go, I will send him to you" (NIV). He told them that through the Holy Spirit the Church would receive power to preach and proclaim the Kingdom of God throughout the world.

The Holy Spirit is referred to as the Spirit of:

- Wisdom (Ephesians 1:17)
- Understanding (Isaiah 11:2)
- Truth (John 14:17)
- Revelation (Ephesians 1:17)
- Prophecy (Revelation 19:10)
- Might (Isaiah 11:2)
- Life (Romans 8:2, Revelation 11:11)
- Knowledge (Isaiah 11:2)
- Holiness (Romans 1:4)
- Grace (Hebrews 10:29
- Glory (1 Peter 4:14)

In addition, we must add the fruit of the Spirit as well! They include: *love, joy, peace, patience, kindness, goodness, faithfulness, gentleness, and self-control*[86] This is the oil God anoints us with. No wonder the oil of gladness displaces mourning. What is left to be sad about?

We should have anticipated this kind of gracious treatment. After all, He provides the perfect table, why wouldn't His anointing be equally as perfect, pleasantly unexplainable, supernaturally energized and wonderfully incomprehensible? Through it He brings provision and joy to us beyond description. The heart of the Psalmist is overwhelmed with wonder and thanksgiving at the Shepherd's gracious love. What is *your* reaction to that same gracious love?

## The Cup

What of the "cup" which overflows? Samuel Burder tells us the custom in the East was not only to anoint guests with a type of fragrant perfume, but also to...

> *"give them a cup of some choice wine, which the host would then carefully fill to the top and then spill over the brim a bit. The anointing of the head was to show their love and respect while the overflowing cup symbolized that while they remained in the house, they would have an abundance of everything. They would be well cared for.*[87]

David's cup was spilling over with God's blessing! Perhaps he couldn't find words adequate enough to express the gratitude of his heart. In his difficulty and overflow of gratitude, all he chose to say to express his joy was, "My cup overflows."

Today, he might say, "My Lord, it is just too much...You are so good to me...there is more than I can contain!" In another Psalm, David said, "Lord, you have assigned me my portion and my cup. You have made my lot secure. The boundary lines have fallen for me in pleasant places. Surely I have a delightful inheritance".[88]

Although David could be referring to what the Lord has done around him, his true treasure is found in his overflowing cup, filled with his heart's desire—the Lord God Himself. David said, "You are my portion".[89] He has set his heart on one love, one goal, and one purpose in life, the Lord God. In another place, he said, "As the deer pants for streams of water, so my soul pants for you, O God. My soul thirsts for God, for the living God. When can I go and meet with God?"[90]

David's heart found its life in the fullness of God, and his cup was overflowing. This position in God is the only explanation for the times David experienced difficulty in life but still declared, "My cup overflows." If we trust in Christ and find our identity in Him, then *our* cup is overflowing as well!

If your heart fails to find its place in Christ, then when negative situations arise, you will find a depleted or empty cup. God knows when we allow Him to fill our hearts—our hearts overflow with Him and we desire nothing else.

## Delight in Him

Psalm 37:4 is a favorite verse that is often quoted and written in personal prayer journals: "Delight yourself in the Lord and He will give you the desires of your heart." Too often we emphasize the latter portion of this verse instead of focusing on the part where David placed *his* greatest emphasis, the part that contains the key for the liberation of hearts.

We all know we should *delight ourselves in the Lord*—it should be our first and highest priority! Yet most of the time, it is not. David knew everything his heart required and desired would be filled to overflowing *when he delighted himself completely in the Lord*.

When you dare to delight yourself in the Lord, every wound and every void in your heart is cared for. When your heart is overflowing with the love of God, every desire to venture outside of His love and kingdom ceases. We clearly see the world's heart remedies as anemic counterfeits! All is fulfilled and overflowing with Him and in Him.

It is our Heavenly Father who *always* gives good gifts to His children. His greatest of all gifts to us is *Himself*. When we are completely enveloped by Him, then our hearts desires are fulfilled.

As we are given to Him, all else grows dim and our cup overflows and we find ourselves declaring with the Psalmist, "Whom have I in heaven but You? And earth has nothing I desire but You".[91]

If you haven't yet discovered this life lived within the Lord; it may sound foreign to you to talk about "a heart consumed by God." *Many* of us have yet to experience the deep impact of these words.

Once you discover this place of fullness, this cup of overflowing in God's presence, you can begin to understand how God's people have faced unthinkable difficulties and persecution because of their faith in total peace and great courage.

In the 1500's, Queen Mary took the throne of England and banished the Gospel of salvation by grace alone. She unleashed a season of horrid persecution against Protestant Christians and anyone else who dared to challenge her authority and decisions.

One of her many innocent victims was a man named John Denley. He was condemned and sentenced to death by burning at the stake unless he recanted his beliefs. He refused, and was taken to the designated area of execution in a public place for all to see as a warning to any who would oppose the Queen.

John was secured to a stake, wood was piled around him and the fire was lit as a crowd looked on. As the flames grew stronger, John began singing a Psalm instead of screaming out for mercy and release.

One of his tormentors became so disgusted and enraged that he hurled a piece of wood at John, striking him on the face. John didn't curse his assailant, but instead broke into tears. He didn't beg to be released, to be rescued from the flames, or even condemn his enemies. He simply said, "Truly you have spoiled a good old song". He then spread his arms out and resumed his singing until he died within the flames.[92]

There is another story more familiar to us, but equal in courage and calm—the story of Stephen in the Book of Acts. He was a man in love with his Savior, a man whose heart was so given to God that all he desired was fulfilled in delighting in the Lord. The Bible says Stephen was full of grace and power, "...*anointed by the oil of the Spirit of God*" and his cup was overflowing.

Not one of the countless scholars, religious lawyers or Pharisees opposing this "table waiter" could outwit or trick him! In fact, the only way this mob was able to seal his fate was to pay or coerce false witnesses to testify against him. They were so desperate that they would do anything to silence Stephen and cut off his life message of salvation through Jesus Christ.

At his mock trial, they could not stand to hear him testify of Jesus any longer and were overcome with rage and anger. In rage the mob rushed on Stephen and began throwing stones to kill him. Stephen responded with this prayer, "Lord Jesus receive my spirit." Then, instead of crying out for the justice of God to fall upon his attackers, he fell to his knees and prayed, "Lord do not hold this sin against them."[93]

The only conceivable and rational explanation for this prayer is that *Stephen's cup was overflowing with the fullness of God*. He delighted himself in the Lord and was anointed with God's oil, the Holy Spirit.

Stop for a moment and think about just who Christ our Shepherd really is. Remember how He sacrificed of Himself to give to us forgiveness and abundant life. How should we respond? Should it not be to fall on our knees with our arms raised, our hearts overflowing with God's abundant graciousness, and from our lips speak as David spoke, "My cup overflows"?

> *"Your throne, O God will last forever and ever; a scepter of justice will be the scepter of Your Kingdom. You love righteousness and hate wickedness; therefore God, Your God, has set you above your companies by anointing you with the oil of joy".*[94]

## Path Markers:

1. *Oil is the biblical symbol of the Holy Spirit, who is our enabler to fulfill the will of God for us on earth.*
2. *Not only has God sent Him to resource all He has called us to do, but God is a giver, providing more than enough, and causing our cups to overflow.*

# CHAPTER NINE

## Goodness and Mercy

*"Surely, goodness and mercy will follow me
all the days of my life"*

can think of few things more calming and relaxing than the sound of a stream trickling from rock to rock as it flows through the natural beauty of a forest-covered canyon.

On my trail map, the spot I had found was nothing more than a line on paper signifying a crossing point over a stream; merely a mark on a page noting where a path crossed to the opposite bank.

Those who visited before me would probably agree that spot along the trail was really nice. (There is *something* to be said for *anyone* willing to invest the time and energy to hike such a long distance to reach that place!)

For most, that place would probably remain simply "the place on the trail map" where you cross over the stream. That *would* have been me, but I was so tired from the walk that I removed my backpack for a little rest and sat down on a boulder in the middle of the creek-bed.

As I caught my breath, I began to notice the activity downstream.

The location is often blanketed with red, yellow, green and brown leaves from the many sweet gum trees in the ravine. Some leaves appear to have been carefully hand-painted on the water's surface, looking almost surreal.

The longer I gazed at the scene, the more I saw. Increasingly varied pockets of beauty began unfold before me in previously veiled detail. They seemed to appear quickly wherever my eyes paused—it was watching the rapid replay of a time-lapse movie of blooming flowers.

Had I merely crossed this stream and walked on without pausing, I wouldn't have noticed the still pool beneath the sweet gum tree with its white bark and roots extending over the stream before dipping below the water's surface.

The sun shone on the water exposing seven or eight sun perch hovering in a foot of water, but just a few inches over a stone covered in light green moss. The interaction of the sunlight with the colors of the perch caused them to shine brilliantly in several assorted tints. (Yes, I know I am having a moment; and you would probably need to be here to fully appreciate the beauty.)

## Paying Attention

My point is focus. As a young boy I worked on a special project to earn a Scouting merit badge that taught me a great deal about focus. I had to place string around a 1-square-foot section on the ground and then list all the objects I found in that area. My first quick glance produced only two items: soil and grass. However, a slower and more careful search produced a far larger harvest of objects, including different soil types, several kinds of grass and weeds, varieties of tiny pebbles, and a good number of little crawling things.

We might easily skip over this passage without pause and reflection, without stillness and contemplation, without allowing the Holy Spirit to illuminate our minds and hearts.

Just as countless hikers had passed quickly from one side of the stream to the other without paying attention to the beauty and detail of the region, it is easy for us to read David's anointed and inspired words while thinking, "That's nice, what a blessing," and move right on by.

Indeed, it is nice and it unveils a great blessing, so let's stop and "gaze" a little longer at this phrase leading to the end of David's divine hymn.

We know that the 23rd Psalm reveals the place of rest and peace resulting from trust. Trust in God is the bridge that spans even the deepest expanse of uncertainty.

On that same hike, I came upon two old footbridges perhaps about a mile apart "as the crow flies." I'd used the first bridge to cross that same creek nearly a year earlier, but on this day I discovered that only a few parts remained of the bridge. Judging by the debris around the area, the bridge was probably destroyed by a flash flood. I saw a 6-foot section resting in the creek bed, wedged between two small boulders— but the rest of the bridge was nowhere to be seen.

The second bridge further downstream was made from the same materials and in the same fashion. Perhaps it was constructed by the very same builders, but it remained strong and intact where it spanned the creek.

Some might see how the first bridge had been totally destroyed, and then doubt the safety of the second bridge. Fear might so grip them they would refuse to use the bridge to cross the creek.

We could cite countless examples to build a strong case for suspicion, doubt and the possibility of failure. We have all been disappointed by products that didn't perform as promised in their strategically marketed commercials. The same might be true of the seemingly endless political promises thrown at the public every year or two. Nearly everyone has been disappointed and disillusioned by failed relationships, and many have even been hurt in church. You would think that is the *last* place one would be wounded, but it happens.

In the face of failure, disappointment, and potential doubt, God tells us to trust in Him. The enemy, on the other hand, will always point to the failed bridges in our lives, hoping to discourage us from trusting in the one bridge across troubled waters who will never fail us.

## Fellow Travelers

David identifies two wonderful traveling companions in this portion of the Psalm 23. God gives you these companions for life, so that whenever you "look over your shoulder," you will find them following you: *goodness* and *mercy*.

Are you walking through uncertain days and unfamiliar surroundings? Look over your shoulder, because goodness and mercy are following you! Have you have lost your ability to reason; have you temporarily relied on your own strength only to discover your growing weakness? Do you now find yourself running to get back on the right path?

Look over your shoulder. I believe you will see goodness and mercy following you.

"Goodness" is defined as the characteristic or quality of being good. That might mean something is beautiful, bountiful, the best, joyful, kindly, loving, merry, and precious (or more). "Mercy" refers to divine kindness, favor and compassion.

Matthew Henry said, "David's hope rises and is flowing from the fountain, pardoning mercy, protecting mercy, sustaining mercy, supplying mercy."[95] The Psalmist is certain goodness and mercy will always be with him for he says "surely" which means "only" or "nothing but" goodness and mercy will follow all the days of his life. A.G. Clarke writes, "Here is assurance that the shepherd's care will be unremitting day by day".[96] Another author says,

> *"Ever more distinctly and with growing enthusiasm (David) has come to realize how unfathomably rich is the blessing of God which rules over his life. Filled with bliss, he has reached the culminating point of his inward happiness. He can no longer be troubled by sad experiences and nothing will be able to separate him from the 'goodness' and 'loving kindness' of God till he finds his eternal rest."[97]*

Psalm 100 contains one of the great songs of thanksgiving in the Bible. It seems to spring from a deep revelation of God's richness poured upon the heart; and its passages reverberate with gratitude. "Shout for joy to the Lord...worship the Lord with gladness...enter His gates with thanksgiving and His courts with praise. Give thanks to Him and praise His holy name. Why? "For the Lord is good and His mercy endures forever".[98]

When God's Word promises something, you can be certain that it will take place. Do you remember the story of David in 1 Samuel 5 as he led his men to the city of Jebus?

The Jebusites were so certain of the strength of their position, and of the impossibility that David's men would ever overtake them, that they mocked his challenge. They said, "You will not get in here: even the lame and the deaf can ward you off!" They thought to themselves, "David will never get in here."

The Jebusites were convinced victory alone awaited them and defeat would come to David and his men. However, the very next word in 1 Samuel 5:7 is "nevertheless." David conquered the city and changed its name to the "City of David."

When God says something is *sure* or *certain*, then it does not matter what the odds look like in the natural. Things will always go as God intends for them to go. I call this God's "nevertheless principle."

If God has said something is going to happen, it does not matter how many say, "No it will not!" God will cause it to happen *nevertheless!* Psalm 23 says if you trust your life to the Shepherd, then goodness and mercy will follow you all the days of your life.

## I Am Going To...

What about all of life's "twists, turns and uncalculated surprises?" When it appears a trial might be overtaking you, try to remember the deeper heart issue you face is the issue of trust. Again, we quote Proverbs: "Trust in the Lord with all of your heart and lean not upon your own understanding."[99]

You should be cautious about declaring that something is "not good" until you know the actual end of the matter! How would you judge whether or not bananas or apples "tasted good and were good for you" if the only samples you had ever eaten were green and unripe? You could mistakenly label all bananas and apples as "not good" simply because you had never waited for the fruit to mature. Hold judgment until you know the end of a matter.

Look at the life of Joseph again, but this time view it as if you don't already know the "good ending" of his story.

Joseph was a good son, a normal seventeen-year-old living with his family and working for his father tending sheep. Then Joseph had a couple of dreams from God about his future, a destiny that would unfold some time in the future. At that point, we would all probably agree this was a "good thing" from God.

If I had been in Joseph's place, I would probably pack a bag the next day, find Pharaoh's palace, knock on his door and say something like, "Hey, I had a couple of dreams from God. I think I need to be put in some position of authority pretty quick!" Then I live happily ever after. (However, the *real* Author of Joseph's life didn't put this in the next chapter of Joseph's life.)

Joseph went another direction. He shared his dreams with his brothers and ended up stripped of his robe, thrown into an empty cistern, and later sold to Midianite merchants for twenty shekels of silver!

I wonder if he thought, *"Hmm, perhaps I should have slept a bit longer the night of the dream and gotten just a few more details?"*

Had God actually given Joseph the details of his journey in those dreams, he might have been tempted to change his identity. Perhaps he would have taken a low-profile job sanding staffs in a local shepherd supply store in some far away city (all in the hope that God would select someone else for all of the "fun and adventure" about to unfold).

How would you judge this story at this juncture? Joseph faces a toss into a cistern, life as a slave, and exotic travel to a foreign place where he knew no one and had no friends. Wouldn't you lean toward declaring this situation as *"not a good thing"*?

After Joseph was sold to Egypt's captain of the guard in charge of the royal prisoners, he received an upgrade on his journey with the "perks" of added favor, trust, and authority. Things seemed to be looking up again.

How seasons can change! Captain Potifer was great, but his wife apparently had read too many cheap romance novels by candlelight. She tried to seduce young Joseph and when he wisely refused her advances, she became insulted. She flew into a rage and falsely accused Joseph of trying to force himself on her.

This led Joseph to the next chapter in his life as a prisoner in the dungeon, with all the time in the world to catch up on his reading and journaling. Once again Joseph's life seemed to deserve the "no good" rating. Yet, we have still not reached the end of the matter.

Some time later, Joseph again receives favor when the warden of the prison gives him "trustee" liberties and favor. Things are improving, but he *is still a convict.*

One day Joseph interpreted the dreams of his fellow inmates, the Pharaoh's former cupbearer and his baker. They, too, are a little down on their luck and potentially facing an early "forced retirement" and "termination" of their life benefits (just making sure you're still with me.) Joseph agreed to the deal on the condition that these men promise to speak to Pharaoh concerning Joseph's unjust situation.

Once the agreement was struck and the dreams were interpreted, one man received good news and the other...

Well, let's just say the Royal Baker wasn't slated for a vacation in Cancun.

True to Joseph's words, the cupbearer was shown clemency and restored to his former position. In his excitement, however, the cupbearer neglects to mention Joseph to Pharaoh, so he spends yet another *two years* in prison. This scenario would probably earn the "thumbs down" prejudgment of a "bad thing" at this point.

The next scene opens with Pharaoh having a dream. This triggers the faulty memory of the royal cupbearer, who mentions Joseph's dream-interpretation abilities. Pharaoh calls upon Joseph to interpret his dream, and there is a turn of events that opens new doors for Joseph. He eventually rises to the Number 2 position in Egypt, commanding all of the affairs of Egypt and answering only to Pharaoh himself.

Thirteen long years passed between the time Joseph received his original dreams and the time they came to pass. Those were long years filled with deep difficulty and unfair treatment, but Joseph finally reached a place of authority, appointed by Pharaoh as governor of the land.

However, it was only after Jacob, struggling with the effects of the famine, sent his other sons to Egypt to buy grain that the prophetic dreams came to pass. The brothers had to bow to the Egyptian governor (whom they did not recognize as Joseph), and ultimately the entire family ended up in Egypt. By the time both dreams eventually came to pass, a total of 22 years had passed by!

Perhaps the most amazing part of this story is Joseph's attitude after enduring so many years of unfair and unjust treatment. He couldn't resist keeping the drama of the moment intact, but his heart was right. He finally revealed his identity to his brothers with the words, "I am your brother Joseph, *the one you sold into Egypt!* [Ouch!] And now, do not be distressed and do not be angry with yourselves for selling me here [even though you *should*], because *it was to save lives that God sent me ahead of you.*"[100]

Years later, when Jacob the family patriarch died, Joseph's brothers were concerned that Joseph might still have ill feelings towards them. He reassured them by saying, "Don't be afraid. Am I in the place of God? You intended to harm me, but *God intended it for good* to accomplish what is now being done..." [101]

What incredible wisdom, resolve, and character is displayed in the life of this great hero of the faith! We should be wise and *never prematurely judge* something as "not good" until the end of the matter is finally reached.

When the Bible says "...surely, goodness and mercy will follow me," realize that God isn't reciting some man-concocted theory or wishful speculation! No, you are reading God's promise of certainty! This promise is not for *some* of the days of our lives, but "*all* the days of our lives."

Isn't this a good reason for us to join the Psalmist in another song when he declares, "Give thanks to the Lord for He is good and His mercy endures forever"?[102]

*The New International Version* of the Bible exchanges the word love for the word mercy:

> "*I will praise You, O Lord, among the nations;*
> *I will sing of You among the people.*
> *For great is Your love (mercy), higher than the heavens;*
> *Your faithfulness reaches to the skies*".[103]

Scripture tells us, "God is love".[104] Since He is love, all of His actions are motivated by love. He is the source and the very essence of love. Therefore, every act He initiates has love as its catalyst. The natural mind may feel discomfort when considering some of the stories we read in the Bible, but we need to consider "trust" again.

In our present natural form, it is just too much to fully comprehend the One who *only* makes decisions and pursues actions based on holy justice motivated by pure and untainted love. However, we must trust Him, for *the end of every matter* in which He is involved in our lives is good and loving.

## The Rest of The Story

I was invited to minister in Pennsylvania during the early stages of the Iraqi engagement. My host pastor picked me up at the airport and dropped me off at a hotel after a quick lunch. The troops had just arrived in Iraq so the nation (including me) tried to monitor the news as much as possible.

As I was unpacking, a local newscaster reported that a soldier from Pennsylvania involved in the Iraqi invasion had been killed in combat, and was the first casualty from Pennsylvania since the war had begun. The news brief was followed with an interview with the soldier's father.

When the pastor picked me up for dinner with his family, he told me he had just been contacted to minister to the same grieving family that had been mentioned on the TV news program.

We didn't talk much more about the situation until Sunday morning, just before the service. The pastor told me the parents and several family members of the deceased soldier would be attending his church that morning.

Once the service began, the pastor recognized the family members and honored their son; and then the entire congregation joined in prayer for them. It was a very emotional and anointed time of ministry.

A short time later, I was introduced and I began to share in worship, ending in a brief time of teaching. An invitation was extended with several coming to recommit or surrender to Christ for the first time.

The service ended and a few minutes later, as the pastor and I were getting into his car, he said, "Did you know the father of the soldier, as well as some other family members who were present today, came forward to give their lives to Jesus?" I said, "No, I had no idea." It moved me very deeply.

I later found out that, before leaving for Iraq, the man's son had spoken of his concern for his dad's spiritual condition. Now, there was no reason to be concerned because the father had surrendered to Christ and dealt with the issue of trust.

Is this how you and I would have orchestrated this situation? Probably not, but it is not wise to judge something as "not good" until the end of the matter is actually reached. The Bible assures us "...that *all things work together for good* to them that love God, to them who are the called according to his purpose" (Romans 8:28, emphasis mine).

Early one morning I stopped at my favorite local coffee shop for a "double short cappuccino to go." I had pulled a "late-nighter" the night before so I was treating myself to a little caffeine boost.

As I stood in a daze at the inside counter, a truck pulled up to the drive-through window. Even in my stupor, I noticed the driver smiling at me, so I managed to nod back, and that was the extent of our communication.

Then I began to think, *That guy really looks familiar....* However, I just could not place him in any mental or historical context. I looked again but he had already received his order and pulled away, so I got my order and turned toward the door to leave.

Just before I reached the door, the guy from the truck entered the shop, walked up to me and said, "Craig, you don't remember me, do you?"

"Well, you look familiar, but to be honest, no."

"I am Michael. I met you 9-or-10 years ago through another guy who goes to your church. In fact, I even visited your church a couple of times and you took me to lunch a couple of times."

My memory was beginning to "jog," but my recollection was still a little vague.

"I remember asking you the second time you took me to lunch, 'Why are you doing this Craig?' And you looked at me and said, 'I am simply planting seeds,' and continued to talk to me about wanting me to connect with God."

Michael went on to say that not long ago after that conversation, he had gotten deeply involved with drugs and his wife had left him. He became a truck driver and for nine years or so, his life consisted of one mess after another.

Were Michael's story to end here, it would probably be declared, "Not a good thing." Yet, once again, this was not the end of the matter.

This man went on to say that during those nine years, he often thought about our lunch conversation. "Several times I'd attempted to fix things on my own, but each attempt was met only by failure. Not until I surrendered everything to Jesus, trusting Him with my life, did my life finally change."

Michael smiled and described his life since he made that decision, and talked about the church he was a part of. He ended his conversation by saying, "When I saw you at the café counter this morning, I just had to tell you my story."

I tried to encourage Michael in the brief time we had together because I had to leave for a meeting, but in the end I was the one who was encouraged. My feet barely touched the ground as I walked across the parking lot to my truck because my heart was so full of joy and thanksgiving for the goodness of God, the Father of Life.

David declared, "Surely [certainly] goodness and mercy shall follow me all the days of my life." I think if I would have glanced over my shoulder that morning, then I would literally have seen goodness and mercy following me! (And I believe Michael would have seen goodness and mercy following him as well.)

Is it a sunny, joyful day? If your trust is in the Lord, then goodness and mercy *are* following you.

Is it a rainy and more solemn day? Goodness and mercy *are* surely still following you.

Don't declare a thing as "not good," and never doubt that goodness and mercy are following you—even when life is difficult. Regardless of your current situation, if God says, "Surely, goodness and mercy will follow," then it is! Perhaps it is time to claim your *"Nevertheless Day!"* just as David did against the Jebusites.

When God declares a thing as *certain*, then it will be good in the end. *Goodness and mercy are following you* this very moment. And if you continue to trust Him, then your holy companions will *continue* to follow you *all the days of your life*.

If your trust is in the Shepherd, "goodness and mercy" will never abandon you. There is no situation grim enough to frighten them away. Goodness and mercy will follow you all of the days of your life.

Perhaps you are thinking: *Sounds good, but perhaps it is simply too good to be completely true. I have just seen so much pain and disappointment in my life.*

How will you know it is untrue unless you step out in *complete trust*? Psalm 34:8 says, "Taste and see that the Lord is good."

You can trust God when He says something, because He is not like us. The Bible says, "God is not a man that He should lie nor a son of man that He should change His mind. Does He speak and then not act? Does He promise and not fulfill?"[105] He loves His children. He loves caring for them, being good to them and doing good for them. We are all special in His eyes.

When my middle son, Micah, was a very young boy, I often told him how special he was to God. In fact, Dianna told me that during one of their conversations, Micah said, *"Dad said I am very special to God."*

As a young boy, Micah believed those words *because he trusted me*.

In Matthew, Jesus said, "If you... though you are evil, know how to give good gifts to your children, how much more will your Father in heaven give good gifts to those who ask Him".[106]

God sees *you* as very special to Him, and He wants to do good and extend mercy to you. Those are *not* my words, they are God's words. So they are flawless. You can trust them. God is forgiving and good, abounding in love to all who call to Him.[107]

> *"For the Lord God is a sun and a shield;*
> *The Lord bestows favor and honor;*
> *No good thing does He with hold*
> *From those whose walk is blameless."* [108]

Have you looked over your shoulder lately? You are being followed. It is Goodness and Mercy.

## Path Markers:

1. *When the Bible says goodness and mercy will follow all the days of our life, we are not reading theory and speculation, but God's promise of certainty.*
2. *We should never declare whether something is good or bad, until the actual end of the matter.*

# CHAPTER TEN

# Home

*"I will dwell in the house of the Lord forever"*

Define "forever" for me please.
*"FOREVER—always, infinity, endlessness....*
If you are brave enough to look in a thesaurus, you will find some fairly long lists of words to read while trying to understand and define the words "eternal" or "eternity." Despite our best attempts to define these terms, in the end, the natural mind usually ends up in a sort of mental cul-de-sac, just staring at a billboard containing a large question mark.

The human brain just does not have the capacity with the given information to truly comprehend, explain or understand "eternity" or "forever." God simply has not supplied sufficient data for us to grasp what these words mean. At the moment, it remains a mystery, a journey begun, but not yet completed.

Whenever we ponder the broad and elusive subject of time, we can all agree on at least a few of its characteristics. As I understand it, Einstein's Theory of Relativity tells us that time can bend and even be stretched or compressed, but time *is* consistent in the sense that it cannot be stopped by human efforts, *and* once a second has passed, it cannot be retrieved. It becomes history.

Admittedly there are *some* situations and circumstances we are subjected to from (forgive me) "time to time" which may seem to at least create the illusion of circumstantial relativity.

For instance, when you spend time with someone or visit a place that you consider important, mesmerizingly interesting, or just plain fun, then time may *seem* to pass far too quickly for you. On the other hand, if you must spend time with someone or visit a place that you categorize as boring...well, time definitely *seems* to slow to a snail's pace.

When your employer sends you out to pick up something and you get stuck in a long checkout lane, the time passes too quickly. If you get stuck in that *same line* after work on your own time to something for your own needs, then it seems the time passes far too slowly!

For the six days you spend at *work*...time drags slowly by. On the six days of your vacation...time zips past way too fast. I think you get the idea.

I overheard some young Christians discussing heaven and eternity. They were excited about their faith, but they weren't so excited about the kind of activity they thought might go on in Heaven. They asked each other, "What will we look like? Will we know each other? Will we appear as young adults or older adults? *Eternity is a long time...what if I get bored?*"

Even though we can't construct a full mental panorama of Heaven, maybe we can apply a few broad strokes to the canvas. Think of a special event in your life or some unique place you once visited with close friends or family. It should be an event, a place, or a time with a person that you really wanted to continue without having to end.

Heaven and eternity are difficult to imagine because we have never experienced a perfect place in a perfect environment with perfect relationships that are all maintained by God the Father, who is Himself perfect in every way. It will be anything *but* boring and monotonous!

## The Place

We traveled a lot early in our ministry, and we really enjoyed it most of the time. One thing Dianna has endured over the years is listening to me romanticize about "what it would be like to live a lifetime" in the places we visited or passed through.

It could be Chicago, Seattle, Washington, D.C., or New York—she knew I would envision reaching out to a large metro area. The same thing happen whenever we passed through small towns or a farmhouse! What would our ministry look like? Who would our friends and neighbors be?

I saw places for storefront church plants or coffee houses for outreach *everywhere*. In Australia, I told Dianna how easy and exciting it would be to settle for a lifetime among the wonderful people there! The trouble was that she had heard *the same thing* in Mexico, Canada, Russia, the Caribbean, throughout Europe, or anywhere in the United States!

We took a summer trip to Alaska recently, and the romantic bug bit me yet again, stimulating my imagination (and irritating my companion). "I wonder what it would be like to live and minister in Sitka or Juneau?" It got worse.

While walking down the main street of Skagway, a small town of less than 900 people settled as a supply point during the Klondike gold rush in the late 1800's. You know what happened.

"There would be a great location for an outreach café...and look at that building across the street. That could easily be converted into a church. What a cool place to live."

If the new heavens and new earth have anything to do with relationships and locations, (and they do), then perhaps I can begin to get a small glimpse of eternity. Through our travels, we have been honored to meet some of God's very special people over the years. We would instantly fall in love with most of these people, and wished we lived in close enough proximity to so we could make a short drive to their home for an evening of fellowship and begin to develop a long, meaningful friendship.

The problem is there is not enough time to build friendships with everyone in our neighborhood—let alone others situated around the nation and beyond.

Eternity, however, is another matter! There are no time constraints in eternity. I can easily see myself staying in a location, building relationships for the equivalent of a hundred years (or a thousand), then moving to another place to repeat the process with an entirely new set of variables! Think of the countless places to explore and soak in, the adventures to experience, and the vast sea of people to meet and interact with—all while experiencing the constant and fully manifested presence of Jesus Christ! Now *that's* heavenly!

Think of all of the conversations with Him, and the worship we offer to Him—worship celebrations of enormous proportions where we honor and exalt God while gazing on His beauty! We will offer Him songs, books, poems, sculptures, paintings, and words from hearts motivated only by holiness, purity and sincerity.

Perhaps we will worship in small groups, in large groups, on glory-lit hillsides and in lush perfect valleys. We could honor Him on golden street corners, in plazas, parks and whatever else will exist in the new heaven and new earth. In that entire expanse, *nothing* will be stained by impurity, and will be nothing omitted or forgotten. This will be a place of absolute perfection, a holy place where all is directed towards glorifying God. This is a place to abide, a place to dwell with God... FOREVER!

Throughout his 23rd song, the Psalmist has moved us to pastures and quiet waters, through valleys, to banquets and blessing, always maintaining the theme of peace and rest that comes from trusting in God's perfect love.

Now he introduces us to an abode so wonderful that it leads the heart to experiential fullness, immeasurable joy, and lasting contentment. This place he has deemed "the house of the Lord."

Picture yourself traveling a winding road through a beautiful forest. On either side of the lane your eyes fall on one meticulously planned and managed landscaped area after another. Around each curve you are introduced to new picturesque settings with manicured lawns, carefully selected floral varieties, shrubs, conifers, and huge deciduous hardwood trees.

Immediately you realize this grand design is the result of an unusually brilliant visionary and artistically creative personality. You are already extremely impressed with all you see, when suddenly the road leads you to a very large open area.

Your emotions now change from being very impressed to feeling awe and astonishment as you see a house of unbelievable proportions and grandeur coming into your view, in front of a backdrop of mountains. "Majestic" is your initial adjective of choice. In all of your travels, you have never seen anything to compare with this house.

This house features four acres of floor space, four stories of fine lumber, limestone, brick, and marble. (And these are only the basic building materials, not the luxurious interior décor and furnishings.)

There are two hundred and fifty rooms, sixty-five fire places, thirty-four master bedrooms, an indoor swimming pool, three kitchens, huge recreation rooms, a library, a banquet hall, a gymnasium, a stunningly decorated entry and hallways, an enormous garden room, plus various buildings surrounding the house including garages and stables.

Gardens surround the entire estate, each with a different theme and placed in the center of a 100,000-acre forest!

It is beautiful, breathtaking, and awe-inspiring—a strategically planned and completed project designed for many to behold and enjoy. With such ingenious engineering, this masterpiece of architecture must be the house of houses!

Wonderful as it sounds, this is *not* the house of the Lord. It is the house built by the late George Vanderbilt, located in North Carolina.[109] Although it would be fun to visit this place for a while or even for a few years, it is still not the place you would want to dwell in "forever."

Recently I was walking on an Ozarks hiking trail that wound its way through a deep ravine when the path began to lead up a steep hill. Out of breath and finally reaching the top, I looked up and saw a clearing with the shell of an old log cabin at its center. The structure was perhaps 25 feet long and about 18 feet wide.

This one-room cabin rested on native rock piers, and the floor consisted of thick, rough planks. Huge hand-hewn logs made up the four walls and that was the extent of the cabin, with the exception of a rock fireplace and front porch.

As I walked to the front of the cabin, I saw an historical marker standing a few feet from the porch. It read, "Built by John Walker who sold it in 1854 to Owen and Jane West." The cabin's picture-like setting in that clearing of trees on top of an Ozark mountain reflected a simpler, less frantic time.

In that era and location, you worked hard, stayed close as a family, were usually home by nightfall, and read by the light of an oil lamp. You might take the horse or wagon to the closest town only a few times a year! For the most part, you lived your whole life on top of the mountain.

Some might see this as an image of the house of the Lord, as a simple, quiet, and peaceful place. I'll admit the cabin did have a peaceful feel as the sun began to set in the west. I wanted to stay and enjoy the cool evening air as it settled on the mountain, and hear the sounds that might unfold in the woods at dusk. However, I needed to get back to the place I was staying that night. Wonderful as it was, it was not a place you would want to dwell in forever.

You see, it is not the shape, size or location of the dwelling that will cause contentment forever. After all, the "New Jerusalem" described in the Book of Revelation is very impressive by our standards—it is very extravagant and difficult to imagine. It is described as being 1,400 miles wide, long and high! This equals the distance from San Diego, California, to the Oklahoma-Arkansas border, or Paris, France to Istanbul, Turkey!

Who, except for God, could imagine a city of such immensity? It will make New York, Paris, London, and Mexico City *combined* seem like an old roadside store with one gas pump, a broken air hose, with Moon-Pies® and RC® Cola as the only things to eat and drink!

Although the House of the Lord will be perfect to the eye, there will be something else that will cause our hearts to desire to dwell there forever.

## The Presence

Gene and Sue Haggard were the first older couple we met after moving to Fort Smith. We were in our early twenties and very excited about our move and the prospect of our first ministry unfolding before us. Gene was a retired Air Force pilot, so it was natural for he and his wife, Sue, to take us under their wing (sorry) almost immediately along with several other young people.

Our divine appointment took place in the parking lot following our first church in our new hometown. For some reason we were one of the last people in the lot, and the Haggards drove up and asked if we would like to go to lunch with them. We gladly accepted, and began what became a long friendship.

The Haggards lived in a Victorian home in Van Buren on Thirteenth Street. Their house was built around the turn of the twentieth century and had been in Mr. Haggard's family for many years.

Gene and Sue loved God, they loved people, they loved to worship and pray, and they seemed to host a continual string of Bible studies, prayer groups and fellowships. They were a constant source of spiritually rich encouragement, joy, counsel and exhortation to us, and to countless other people.

They always seemed to be inviting someone into their home or helping someone in need. They had a gift for making you feel wanted, accepted and loved. We were always excited when they extend an invitation to us to spend some time with them in their home.

As I look back on those years I have often thought, *"Surely they grew weary of always having people like us around so much."* Yet, if they did feel that way, they never revealed it.

We enjoyed many late-night fellowships in their den or living room, sometimes on the front porch in summer. We enjoyed early morning coffee and conversation around their kitchen table. Everyone knew that if they couldn't make it home for the holidays, it was no problem—there was always room for a few more people around the Haggard table! Whenever you visited their house, you sensed friendship, refuge, and encouragement.

What made the Haggard house a place so loved by so many? And why did we all want to visit that house so often? Was it the architecture, the large yard, the wonderful interior design or location? No, of course not!

Everyone was drawn to that *wonderful, hospitable, loving Southern couple* that lived in the Haggard house! At one point, the Haggards decided to sell their house in Van Buren and move to some acreage in the countryside that had been in the family for years. They eventually built a house there, but for quite some time they lived in a small mobile home.

You probably know what happened already. That mobile home became the new sought-out refuge for many! Why? It is because *that* is where the *Haggards* lived.

It is the *host* of a house that causes it to be a desired dwelling place, not the dwelling itself. Once the Haggards moved, we no longer felt drawn to their old beautiful Victorian home. I have driven past it many times through the years, but all it does is stimulate memories! The house itself has no drawing power.

Even the home were we live now, the place we've called home for about twenty years, is *just a place*—wonderful as it is and as thankful as we are for it as God's blessing and provision. It would only be a place to get in out of the rain if you it weren't for the life reflected through the Smith family that resides there.

## His House

The Bible constantly refers to the "House of the Lord" or the "House of God." The implication is always to the temple or the sanctuary, to the place where the people of God met for worship.

Whatever it may look like in the future, of this we can be sure: God's house will be filled with the presence of the Lord. It's life and light will come from our heavenly Host who has invited and is preparing us to abide there forever. It isn't the structure or the location itself! We will behold *His face* and abide in *His presence*.

It is no wonder that the Psalmist proclaimed with a full and grateful heart, "One thing I ask of the Lord, this is what I seek; that I may dwell in the house of the Lord all the days of my life, to gaze upon the beauty of the Lord and to seek Him in His temple."[110]

David says he will dwell *"in"* the house of the Lord forever. He will not be a wandering pilgrim forever, he will dwell in and reside in that house. He will not stand outside or peer through a window, curiously wondering what it would be like to live inside. He will forever be an inhabitant because he has trusted his life to his Shepherd, his King and his God. His heart has arrived at the place of permanent residence within the house of the Lord and it will be his dwelling place forever.

## Kindertransport

On November 18, 1938, Britain authorized an operation known as Kindertransport, in response to the growing persecution of the Jews in Germany under Hitler's regime. It's goal was to relocate as many Jewish children as possible from Germany, Austria, and Czechoslovakia to safe foster homes in England.

Some 10,000 children were rescued from Hitler's demonic plan for world conquest and ethnic cleansing.

Try to imagine the pain felt by parents as they took their most precious possessions—their children—to train stations knowing they would probably never see them again.

Many parents told their children they would join them a few weeks later, and others told their children they were being sent on a holiday or vacation. Each child was allowed one suitcase, a small carry-on bag, and a little money. Each was issued a number that was placed on a plain card and hung around the child's neck with string.

Most departed by train to European ports on the English Channel, where they transferred to boats or ships for passage to London.

The final parting at the train stations must have been confusing and emotionally painful; especially for the parents. They knew of the growing and impending dangers awaiting those who remained in regions under Hitler's growing influence. They could only hope their children would have a better chance for life and a future by escaping to England.

Around 300 Jewish children arrived each day in London. Most had sponsors, but those who did not were sent to temporary camps until sponsors could be found. Unfortunately, some children moved from sponsor to sponsor, leaving many of them with additional emotional trauma from multiple relocations.

Within a few months after the transport began, the children who were placed with families in London had to be relocated again because of Hitler's imminent threat to bomb London. This only increased the stress caused by unfamiliar surroundings, uncertainty and emotional insecurity.

Tragically, most of those children lost their parents to the insanity of Hitler's holocaust. In a film documentary of this incident, one woman recalling her ordeal said, "I never belonged when I was a child, I wanted roots."[111]

## Hannah's Story

A few years ago, my wife and I were part of a conference in Phoenix, Arizona, with a focus on ministering to unreached people groups in the world. During the conference, we met and befriended the Mileys. It turned out that Hannah Miley was one of the 10,000 children rescued through the Kindertransport operation.

Hannah was a very happy, normal little girl living in Gemund, Germany, with her parents. They loved her very much and supplied her with a wonderfully secure home environment until she was seven years old. Throughout those years, Hitler's influence was growing and life was changing and growing darker in her city. Due to the wisdom and protection of her parents, Hannah was protected and not very aware of the growing danger.

Seeing no alternative to the unfolding gloom, her parents decided to remove Hanna from danger, and they began laying the groundwork for what Hannah thought was just going to be simply "a nice trip."

It was a warm July evening in Gemund when Hannah and her parents departed for the train station. There were many parents and children moving through the station, but with few exceptions, the only people boarding the train were children. Hannah suspected nothing up to this point other than that she was going on the "nice trip" her parents had prepared for her.

Only after she was placed on the train steps and saw her mother in tears did she realize something was wrong. Suddenly fear and uncertainty intruded on their final goodbye, and deep concern flooded her mind. She knew something was very wrong.

As the train departed, most of the children were running up and down the aisles of the passenger car as though they were participating in some sort of game—but Hannah sat quietly, still and withdrawn. After the train ride and ship passage across the channel, she found herself standing in a holding area in a London train station, listening to an unfamiliar language spoken all around her.

She knew no one. Nor did she have any idea of where her trip would end or where her eventual dwelling place would be. She watched adult sponsors take one child after another away from the detaining area until only she and five others remained.

Hannah was tired, sleepy, and still uncertain about her final destination, uncertain when the next stage of her journey began. The remaining children were placed in a car and driven from location to location. At each stop, adults approached the vehicle, looked over the children, made a selection and then led a child away. The process continued from one stop to the next until each child had been placed with a sponsor, including Hanna.

She was a little seven-year-old Jewish girl who had grown up under the love, care, and protection of her devoted parents, but she felt only... "Isolation...I was plucked out of an environment of love and placed in a no-man's-land. I didn't know English, where I was or who I was with."[112]

After a brief season with the sponsors who had selected her from the car on that first night in England, things changed again. Her sponsors decided things were not working out and she was moved to a second home, and would have to adapt to yet another new environment.

Hannah lost her home, her parents, and her sense of security. Years later, she would learn that her parents had died in the Holocaust, along with other family members and friends.

The years passed, the war ended, and Hannah constantly tried to adjust to her surroundings. She eventually learned English and attended a teachers' college, but in her heart she never really found the dwelling place she longed for. She described her feelings "as dark" and having a desperate need for a loving family.

Although her second set of sponsors were rigid and legalistic, she did benefit from being made to read the Bible consistently. At one point, she realized she "had a need for God, and that Jesus Christ was the bridge to God."

In 1961, she was invited to attend a radio relay service of an American evangelist who was ministering in England. She accepted the invitation and joined a number of others one evening who gathered at a local Church of England to hear the broadcast. Hanna listened intently to the evangelist and even remembers the scripture text he used that evening from Acts 17:30: "In the past God overlooked such ignorance, but now He commands all people everywhere to repent."

When the sermon ended and the evangelist, a young American named Billy Graham, extended the invitation for those listening to repent of their sin and trust in Jesus Christ as their Lord and Savior, Hannah became a believer in Jesus, and placed her life into His care.

She said, "I did not experience love from the time I left my parents until I met Christ and received His love...and His is such a deeper love."

Finally, after her long journey, Hanna's heart found its dwelling place and she could echo the words of David the Psalmist with a full and thankful heart, "I will dwell in the House of the Lord forever."

One August my wife and I found ourselves in the small German village of Gemund, with Hanna and her husband George who were ministering there. The Miley's have traveled to and from Germany for several years, taking groups to pray in the region and to establish a new ministry there.

One day we were privileged to walk several of the streets in and around the village as Hanna described what her life was like there as a little girl.

The place that once held only sad memories for Hannah's cruelly interrupted life has now become a place for which she has a great love and burden. Through God's grace, she was drawn back to her childhood village where some of the residents still remember the plight of Hannah and her parents.

God has given Hannah a tremendous love for the residents in Gemund and the surrounding area. She is building relationships and sharing the story of God's miraculous capacity to heal and fill a heart once hopeless and wounded.

## The Promise

God invites all of us to receive Him as our Shepherd, Savior, Lord, King and Friend. It is through trusting Him that rest comes, even in the midst of trials and hardships. This is His promise, and He deeply desires to walk with us through each step of our lives.

F. B. Meyers said that if we allow God to be our Lord, if we follow and trust Him, then our lives will:

> *"...shape (themselves) into a Psalm, like that which David sang so long ago. It may begin with the tale of the shepherd's care for a lost and truant sheep. But it will not stay ever on that level: it will mount and soar and sing near Heaven's gate, it will spend its days on the level of those shining table-lands where God Himself is Sun; and it will finally pass into that holy and glorious Home-circle, each inhabitant of which may affirm without the least shadow or presumption of fear. "I will dwell in the House of the Lord forever."*[113]

Every believer will come to a transitional point some day when his or her mission as a pilgrim on this earth will close. We will no longer see just a poor mirror-like reflection of the Lord, but we will see the High and Holy One to which we have prayed, worshipped, and proclaimed, and we will behold Him "face to face."[114] We will dwell with Him in His house...FOREVER!

> *"But I, by Your great mercy will come into Your house;*
> *in reverence will I bow down toward Your holy temple."*[115]

## Path Markers:

1. *Though difficult to understand, eternity and heaven are a reality.*
2. *What will make heaven a desired place for eternity and our home will be the constant presence of God our Savior*

# CHAPTER ELEVEN

## First Steps

As I write these final words to you, a low faint rumble is all that lingers from a predawn thunderstorm. Light steady raindrops are falling on the steep pitched roof. I can hear them rolling down the shingles, gathering in the metal gutter, flowing to the downspout and drumming a steady rhythm as the drops contact the curved metal bottom spout just outside the sunroom door.

The over cast skies and surrounding woodlands are creating gray-green, dimly lit hues for the unfolding of the morning. The intense grip of several weeks of summer's hot, stale and dusty air has been replaced by the fresh and cool breeze of the late-August early morning shower. I, for one, welcome the cool breeze like the visit of a favorite old friend.

Outside the window, the falling raindrops form coin-sized bubbles on the surface of a water puddle, but they vanish as quickly as they appeared. The heart-shaped leaves on the Redbud tree glisten and shimmer with moisture and new life as the shower brings relief to the dull, dry look of yesterday.

This is a long and steady rain that is soaking and saturating the soil. Its overflow is gathering in puddles, encircling the crate myrtle, ash and river birch trees; and streaming under the hostas, caladiums, and zinnias.

A little gray tree frog clings to the corner of the downspout in a small space between the bricks and guttering, sheltering itself from the rain (and perhaps hoping for a passing insect for morning breakfast). A tiny green "spring peeper" has found haven within a fire red azalea bush pressing against the narrow levered window.

And so I end this writing where it began—in the sunroom of our home, the place I call the "Barnabas Room." (Barnabas means "Son of

Encouragement.") When we added it to our house several years ago, we wanted it to be a place that did just that—encouraging others and us as well.

Once again, I am enjoying a rare moment of solitude. I see and sense countless things that await discovery, but so often remain in the shadows because stillness, calm, and quiet are so rarely visited when I'm on the fast track. These are places prepared for me by God, but like remote and romantic destinations on the cover of exotic travel magazines, they often remain as elusive and recluse as if I could *never* visit them, or as if they didn't exist at all.

Last night while standing around chatting in a friend's kitchen, I looked to my right and saw a calendar tacked to the end of a row of cabinets. I was still listening to those talking, but I sidled over a couple of steps until I was standing in front of the calendar. That was when I began to stare at the beautiful photo of a castle above the month of August.

The conversations continued around me, but I began thinking about how wonderful it would be to visit the castle in the photo. Then I had that familiar feeling come over me, the one you feel when you begin to recognize that was buried in some distant part of your memory. Warm thoughts began to unfold in me as I realized *I knew this place.*

Then I read the small print at the bottom of the photo, "The Castle at Cochem." "Dianna, come here and look at this!"

We had spent a couple of days in this little village on the Mosel River, a few years earlier while visiting Europe. The balcony from our hotel room had a wonderful view of the castle from the opposite side of the river.

The morning after we arrived, we enjoyed breakfast in a dining room with windows overlooking the township and then ventured to the other side of the river. We walked through several steep and narrow winding streets, passed through a small hillside vineyard, and finally approached the stone-covered entrance of our destination to tour our first castle.

I felt a surge of fond thoughts that I hadn't experienced in years. It was almost like visiting the place again. I could feel the warmth of the sun and hear the shop owners speaking in German as they spread tablecloths on the tables in their quaint cafes and restaurants.

Once again, my memories strolled down narrow cobblestone streets lined with beautiful buildings of Bavarian architecture. We passed by several small family-owned bakeries with pastry-filled windows, producing near-heavenly scents drifting from their open doors to tempt passersby.

After a full day and an evening meal on a balcony restaurant overlooking the river and the shops below, we returned over the Mosel River bridge at sunset as an evening breeze cooled the valley that was home to the village of Cochem.

All that from a few seconds *gazing at a calendar photo*!

I've learned that quieting myself in the presence of the Lord has much the same effect. Once I settle in and settle down, I experience a return of the thoughts and feelings of all that is right, good, and encouraging. The seemingly elusive peace we all long for is not discovered in some far away location. The soul's calm return is centered in the trust of a Shepherd and King.

My heart was fashioned for this place. When I remain here, my spirit is realigned and restored. I should visit this place often, but I confess it is more difficult to consistently sustain my stay here than any other.

However, I never quit the pursuit! It is absolutely necessary for my spiritual health and the accomplishing of God's goals. The moment I quiet myself, acknowledge His presence, and listen to and follow the Shepherd, then I am quickly ushered into the place of my chief desire, fulfillment, peace, discovery, and life! It is the place found only in the presence of Jesus.

There is a frayed and worn cliché that often used, but it nevertheless contains truth and encouragement for your response to David's 23rd Psalm: *"Every journey begins with a first step."*

Don't embrace remorse too long over all the time lost. Don't think you are unworthy. Simply change your plans. Put this *first* on the list— Make the Lord your Shepherd, He is the lover of your soul! Follow Him and He will lead you, provide for you, protect you, and prepare a divine banquet for you! He has provided everything you need to successfully live the Christian life in a world desperately searching for a Shepherd.

# PSALM XXIII

The Lord's my shepherd; I'll not want;
He makes me to lie down
In pastures green; He leadeth me
The quiet waters by.

My soul He doth restore again,
And me to walk doth make
Within the paths of righteousness
Even for His own Name's sake

Yea though I walk in death's dark vale
Yet will I fear none ill,
For Thou art with me, and Thy rod
And staff me comfort still.

My table Thou hast furnished
In presence of my foes;
My head Thou dost with oil anoint,
And my cup overflows.

Goodness and mercy all my life
Shall surely follow me,
And in God's house for evermore
My dwelling-place shall be.

*From the Scottish Metrical Psalter of 1650. A revision by Nichol Grieve, M.A., T&T Clark, Edinburgh, 1940.*

# "THE CHRISTIAN'S SHEPHERD"

The Lord my pasture shall prepare
And feed me with a shepherd's care
His presence shall my wants supply
And guard me with a watchful eye
My noonday walks he shall attend
And all my midnight hours defend.

When in the sultry glebe I faint
Or on the thirsty mountains pant
To fertile vales and dewy meads
My weary wandering steps he leads
Where peaceful rivers soft and slow
Amid the verdant landscapes flow

Though in a bare and rugged way
Through devious, lonely wilds I stray
His bounty shall my pains beguile;
The barren wilderness and smile,
With lively greens and herbage crowned,
And Streams shall murmur all around.

Though in the paths of death I tread
With gloomy horrors overspread
My steadfast heart shall fear no ill,
For Thou, O Lord, art with me still
My friendly crook shall give me aid
And guide me through the dismal shade.

*From Isaac Watts, Select Hymns, 1856, titled "The Christians Shepherd," by Addison.*

# The Village2Village Story

*Village2Village, connecting those who need
help with those who can help.*

*"They went out and traveled from village to village, proclaiming
the good news and healing everywhere."*                    *Luke 9:6*

*"For I was hungry and you gave me something to eat, I was
thirsty and you gave me something to drink, I was a stranger
and you invited me in, I needed clothes and you clothed me, I
was sick and you looked after me, I was in prison and you came
to visit me."*                                      *Matthew 25:35-36*

Village2Village was birthed in February 2010 while I was spending a few days alone in a small 10X14 foot cabin about two hundred yards from the Belize River in the tiny community of Banana Bank. It was not my first mission trip or visit to another country because I have made several such trips over the years, but for some reason this one had an unusual effect on me. One rainy morning I was sitting at a small table writing some thoughts in a notebook, when the sound of the drops hitting the tin metal roof began to subside. As it did I put my pen down, looked up through the small window and watched a color-ful tropical bird land on the branches of a nearby tree. In the distance was the voice of a male Howler monkey letting others that may be in the area know that he was the territorial authority and willing to meet challengers if necessary.

While gazing through the window I began to think of the people I had seen the couple of days before as I was escorted by a missionary to visit several small villages. I saw the smiles of small children tossing coconuts, playing soccer with a make shift ball of some kind, huts with dirt floors, bamboo poles for walls, and palm leaf roofs. Metal grates placed over stones for open fire cooking inside the huts. People bath-ing, playing, and cleaning clothes in streams and rivers, then hauling water in containers back along dusty roads and paths, to their dwellings. The names of More Tomorrow, San Pablo, Dump, Valley of Peace, or even Belmopan the country's capitol city were only places I had heard one missionary speak of. Now those villages had faces and situations attached to them.

I felt I wanted and needed to attempt to do more than just help support the few missionaries our church was assisting. I knew we had stretched our churches mission budget about as much as we could and yet there were so many more genuine sincere worthy people I knew that needed and could use help. That is when in my mind the "What Ifs'" began to materialize and make their presence known.

- "What if I could do and be more involved somehow?"
- "What if I could use what influence I might have to help raise the awareness, and support of missionaries I know and I am getting to know?"
- "What if I could begin to network friends and acquaintances not currently connected or involved in missions and helping others in the mission field and get them interested and involved also?"
- "What if we could begin to make products available the profits of which would go to assist those working to help others and the people and projects they are engaged in?"
- "What if a growing community of friends developed focused on helping others?"

I realize there are many organizations doing the same or similar thing as Village2Village, but there is still plenty of need in our world. The need is actually so overwhelming; many do not know where to begin or which group to support. Village2Village is merely building a community of people linked together to do our part with the people we are already in relationship with and people we are building relationship with.

## Current Projects

### Ganda, Uganda:

V2V is currently involved in Ganda, Uganda where a new building for the students of Grace Kindergarten and Primary School is being constructed. The first floor is finished and once completed the school will accommodate 300 children. We are assisting our friend and indigenous pastor Nsimbi George. His vision is to serve Christ by serving the people in the region in which he lives. The school began with a few children but has quickly grown to over 150 young students with many others desiring to attend as they see the opportunity to better themselves through a Christian education.

In addition to the skills they are learning, the meal the students receive each day is often their best for the day, which often is a bowl of rice and beans, and chicken when possible. We are hoping to complete the school, remodel a church nearby, and complete a center in the village which will not only inspire hope, but provide the equipping tools to see it materialize.

## Belmopan, Belize:

In Belmopan, V2V is assisting Lee Brockinton and his family who moved from Houston, Texas where they pastored a growing church of 400 people. He sensed God leading them to move to Belize to begin planting churches. In February 2014 they will have been on the ground there for 2 years. In that time the church has grown to over 200. They have small groups throughout the region, one reaching students at the University of Belize and plan to soon begin a church in the village of Maya Mopan just outside Belmopan. In the meantime they have built a small home for one of the villagers and some 30 to 40 people are meeting there mid-week for Bible study. Three additional small homes for villagers in Maya Mopan are being completed as well.

## Village2Village Hope Centers

The long term goal and vision of Village2Village is to establish sustainable, reproducible Hope Centers for the purpose of inspiring the hearts of those living within the region of a center with the possibility of genuine transformation and a hopeful future through education, application, and supplemental resourcing. The two proto types are currently targeted for Africa and Central America.

Please prayerfully consider helping us with this vision by visiting www.village2village.co and making a tax-deductible financial contribution today.

# NOTES

1 Alan Greenspan, The Age of Turbulence"
2 The Shepherd Psalm, F.B. Meyer, Christian Lit. Crusade, 1972, Ft. Washington, PA., 19034, p. 11
3 C.H. Spurgeon, "The Treasury of David", Vol. I, Part 1, p.353, MacDonald Pub. Co., McClean, Va. 22102
4 The Shepherd Psalm, F.B. Meyer, Christian Lit. Crusade, 1972 Ft. Washington, PA 19034, p.11

## Chapter One: The Lord is my Shepherd

5 Jeremiah 29:13
6 Gen 48:15,NIV
7 Isaiah 40:11
8 John 10:14
9 Isaiah 40:18,25
10 James M. Boice, "Psalms" 1-41, p. 207, Vol. 1
11 Isaiah 46:9,10
12 Acts 17:24 NIV
13 Psalm 27:1
14 Phil. 4:19 NIV
15 John 6:35
16 Psalm 145:13
17 Psalm 121:8

## Chapter Two: The Green Pastures and Quiet Waters

18 F.B. Meyer, the Shepherds Psalm, p. 22, 1972, Christian Lit. Crusade, Ft. Washington, PA 19034
19 Ibid

20  Proverbs 16:9
21  John 10:14

## Chapter Three: The Restoration

22  F.B. Meyer, p. 27
23  Isaiah 40:31
24  Psalm 33:4
25  Henry Blackaby, "Experiencing God", Blackaby and Claude King, p. 36, Broadman and Holman Pub., 1994
26  Colossians 1:16,17
27  Oz Guiness, "the Call", W. Pub. Group, p. 31, 1998
28  Psalm 27:14
29  Psalm 41:3
30  Zechariah 4:6
31  Matthew 11:28-30

## Chapter Four: The Paths of Righteousness

32  Isaiah 55:12
33  Matthew Henry Commentary, II Corinthians, p. 636
34  Second Epistle of Paul to the Corinthians, R.V.G. Tasker, Tyndale, New Testament Commentaries, p. 142
35  Psalm 33:7 New Living Translation, Tyndale House Publishers, Inc. Wheaton, Il.1997.
36  Isaiah 35:8
37  Book of Isaiah, Edward J. young, p. 454, NI Comm. Eerdmans, 1969
38  Psalm 119:105
39  Psalm 119:11(NASV)
40  Psalm 143:8
41  Psalms 37:23-25
42  Psalm 12:6, Psalm 18:30

## Chapter Five: Valley of the Shadow

43  John 15:14,15 (NIV)
44  Proverbs 3:5 (NIV)
45  Hebrews 13:5 (NIV)
46  Matthew 28:20 (NIV)

47 Romans 8:26,27

48 Hebrews 7:24,25

49 Revelation 21:4 (NIV)

50 "The New Foxes Book of Martyrs", John Foxe, updates by Harold J. Chadwick, Bridge Logos Pub., North Brunswick, N.J. 1997, p. 351

## Chapter Six: Comfort

51 60 Minutes II, Interview with President Bush, 9-10-2003 by Scott Pelley

52 Isaiah 66:13 (NIV)

53 F.B. Meyer, The Shepherds Psalm, Christian Lit. Crusade, Ft. Washington, PA 19034, 1972, p. 46

54 USA Today, Wed. Aug. 20th, 2003 p. 8, section A

55 As told by Tim xxx, Pastor, First Assembly of God, St. Joseph, MO

56 Homelife in Bible Times, p. 19, Arthur W. Klinck, 1947, Concordia Publishing House, St. Louis, Mo.

57 The Treasury of David, Vol. 1, Part 1, p. 368, MacDonald Pub. Co., McLean, VA 22102

58 A Shepherd looks at Psalm 23, Phillip Keller, 1970, p. 94 Zondervan Pub., 24th printing, April 1976

59 Psalms 73:4,5 (NIV)

60 Psalm 73:12 (NLT)

61 Psalms 73:13,14 (NLT)

62 Psalms 73:23,24,26 (NIV)

63 Psalms 73:27,28 (NIV)

64 Hebrews 12:7 (NIV)

65 Hebrews 12:11 (NIV)

66 Psalm 119:75

67 Acts 13:22

68 Strong's Exhaustive Concordance of the Bible, James Strong, MacDonald Pub. Co., p.112

69 A. Graham Scroggie, "Psalms", Flemming, Revel Co., Old Tappan, N.J. 1948, p. 147

## Chapter Seven: The Table

70 Gerald H. Wilson, NIV Application Commentary, Psalm Vol. 1 (Grand Rapids: Zondervan, 2002) p.436

71  International Standard Bible Encyclopedia Vol. 5 (Grand Rapids: Eerdmans Publishing, 1939( p.2898

72  F.B. Meyer, The Shepherd Psalm (Ft. Washington: Christian Literature Crusade, 1972) p.53

73  Acts 17:24-28

74  Jeremiah 10:6

75  Gerald H. Wilson, NIV Application Commentary, Psalms, Vol. 1 (Grand Rapids: Zondervan, 2002) p.436

76  Psalm 31:19, 20 NLT

77  Psalm 16:11

78  Unchained Memories (Boston: Bulfinch Press, 2002) p.114

## Chapter Eight: Overflowing Favor

79  ISBE, p. 138 W.B. Eerdmans Pub. Co., Grand Rapids, MI, 1939, Vol. IV

80  A Shepherd Looks at Psalm 23, Phillip Keller, p. 116

81  Keil & Delitzsch Comm. on the Old Test., p. 23, computer

82  Psalm 104:15 (NIV)

83  Isaiah 61:3

84  "Psalms, A.G. Clarke, Kregal Pub., Grand Rapids, MI, 1979, p. 80

85  "What the Bible says about the Holy Spirit", Stanley Horton, Gospel Publishing House, Springfield,Mo. 65802, 1976, p. 42

86  Galatians 5:22 (NIV)

87  Samuel Burder, "The Treasury of David", vol. 1 McDonald Pub. Co., p. 371, McClean, Va. 22102 by Charles Spurgeon

88  Psalms 16:5,6 (NIV)

89  Psalm 119:57 (NIV)

90  Psalms 42:1,2 (NIV)

91  Psalm 73:25 (NIV)

92  Foxes Christian Martyrs of the World, 1985, Barbour and Co., Inc., 164 Millstreet, Westwood, NJ, 07675, p. 134

93  Acts 7:59 (NIV)

94  Psalms 45:6,7 (NIV)

## Chapter Nine: "Surely, Goodness and Mercy will follow me all the days of my life"

95  Matthew Henry Comm., Vol. III, p. 318

96  A.G. Clarke, p. 80, Kregel Pub., Grand Rapids, MI., 49501, 1979

97 The Psalms, Arthur Weiser, Westminister Press, 1962, Phil., PA,
   p. 230
98 Psalm 100:5 (NIV)
99 Proverbs. 3:5
100 Genesis 45:4, 5
101 Genesis 50:19, 20
102 Psalm 107:1
103 Psalms 108:3,4
104 I John 4:16
105 Numbers 23:19 (NIV)
106 Matthew 7:11
107 Psalm 86:5
108 Psalm 84:11 (NIV)

## Chapter Ten: "I Will Dwell in the House of the Lord Forever"

109 Adapted, "A guide to the Biltmore Estate (centennial edition), The
    Biltmore Pub. Co., One North Park Square, Ashville, NC, 28801, 1994
110 Psalm 27:4
111 Kindertransport Doc., W.B. "Into the Arms of Strangers", "Stories of
    the Kindertransport" 2000, Warner Brothers, 4000 Warner Blvd.,
    Burbank, CA 91522
112 From an interview with Hanna Miley.
113 The Shepherd Psalm, F.B. Meyers, Christian Literature Crusade, Ft.
    Washington, PA, 19034, pp. 90,91, 1972
114 I Corinthians 13:12
115 Psalm 5:7